Hallelujah Moments

Hallelujah Moments

Finding Joy in the Journey

Jane Lynn Simmons

Copyright © 2013 Jane Lynn Simmons.

All rights reserved. No part of this book may be used or reproduced by any means, graphic, electronic, or mechanical, including photocopying, recording, taping or by any information storage retrieval system without the written permission of the publisher except in the case of brief quotations embodied in critical articles and reviews.

Scripture quotations marked THE MESSAGE are used by permission of NavPress Publishing Group. Copyright © by Eugene H. Peterson 1993, 1994, 1995, 1996, 2000, 2001, 2002.

Scripture quotations marked (NLT) are taken from the Holy Bible, New Living Translation, copyright ©1996, 2004, 2007 by Tyndale House Foundation. Used by permission of Tyndale House Publishers, Inc., Carol Stream, Illinois 60188. All rights reserved.

Scripture quotations marked (NIV) are taken from the Holy Bible, New International Version, NIV. Copyright © 1973, 1978, 1984, 2011 by Biblica, Inc.™ Used by permission of Zondervan. All rights reserved worldwide. www.zondervan.com The "NIV" and "New International Version" are trademarks registered in the United States Patent and Trademark Office by Biblica, Inc.™

Scripture quotations marked (NCV) are taken from the New Century Version®. Copyright © 2005 by Thomas Nelson, Inc. Used by permission. All rights reserved.

WestBow Press books may be ordered through booksellers or by contacting:

WestBow Press
A Division of Thomas Nelson
1663 Liberty Drive
Bloomington, IN 47403
www.westbowpress.com
1-(866) 928-1240

Because of the dynamic nature of the Internet, any web addresses or links contained in this book may have changed since publication and may no longer be valid. The views expressed in this work are solely those of the author and do not necessarily reflect the views of the publisher, and the publisher hereby disclaims any responsibility for them.

Any people depicted in stock imagery provided by Thinkstock are models, and such images are being used for illustrative purposes only.

Certain stock imagery © Thinkstock.

ISBN: 978-1-4497-9242-8 (sc)
ISBN: 978-1-4497-9211-1 (e)

Library of Congress Control Number: 2013907213

Printed in the United States of America.

WestBow Press rev. date: 04/25/2013

In memory of
Mother and Daddy
You gave me wings and taught me to
soar . . . thank you with all my heart.

Uncle Dick
You were my hero from the day I was born.

For
Cole, Emma, Austin, Kailie, Caitlyn, and Rileigh
May our family's legacy of love and compassion
live in your hearts, reflect in your actions, and
bring joy to all you encounter . . . always.

Table of Contents

Introduction ix

Chapter 1	Celebrate! 1
Chapter 2	Fear Not 11
Chapter 3	A Gridiron Analogy for Life 23
Chapter 4	Shamed by the Weak 51
Chapter 5	Rejoice 65
Chapter 6	Packing for the Journey 73
Chapter 7	Out of the Mouths of Babes 87
Chapter 8	Whom Do You Trust? 95
Chapter 9	The Hope of Heaven 105
Chapter 10	In Memoriam 119

Conclusion 139

Acknowledgments 143

About the Author 145

Introduction

I hope that all who read this book will recognize it as a labor of great love. It is a means to share just a few of the stories of people and incidents that have shaped my life in the sincere hope that, through those stories, the readers will be drawn into closer relationship with the Lord they love or be introduced to Him for the very first time. My most fervent prayer is that the contents of this book will be a source of encouragement, inspiration, and hope to all who read it.

The "Another Step Further" sections found at the end of each chapter will challenge you to prayerfully consider what your next step will be in taking the spiritual principles discussed within these pages and making them living, active, essential parts of your life. Simply reading this book may uplift you for a moment, but I would sincerely ask that you take what has encouraged or inspired you and apply the principles therein to your everyday life. It is my fondest desire that this book will prompt significant changes in attitudes and outlooks and that the result of those changes will be a people who boldly reflect the incredible love of their Savior to a hurting world.

True Christianity, true faith in our God and Father, true gratitude to Jesus for all He has done for us, demands that we share compassion, generosity, and unconditional love with all whom He places in our path. Hopefully within these pages you will find the courage and the motivation to do just that.

Chapter One

Celebrate!

Celebrate God. Sing together—everyone! All you honest hearts: raise the roof!
—Psalm 32:11 (MSG)

The unconditional love and genuine acceptance that Steve and Lisa had for their little son, Erik, was obvious the first time I met them in my role as the disabilities ministry director of my church. I knew right away that this was a remarkable family. While keenly aware of his disabilities, Steve and Lisa saw Erik for exactly who he was—not a kid with microcephaly, cerebral palsy, and a seizure disorder, but a very special little boy created with a delightful personality and a unique purpose for his life. Steve and Lisa accepted and loved their son without conditions. They rejoiced in their son, but at the time we met,

Steve had no idea that he himself had a Creator, a heavenly Father, that rejoiced in him as well.

As Steve witnessed the love and support that was lavished on his little family through the volunteers and staff of our disabilities ministry, the love of our heavenly Father became real to him for the first time. Steve was radically and dramatically changed in the light of God's love. His love for Lisa was a love that protected, supported, and encouraged even more than before. It was love based on respect and rooted in selflessness. Once Steve learned about it, He clearly followed the apostle Paul's admonition to the Christian men of Ephesus by loving Lisa just as Christ loved the church. Steve became one of the best examples I have ever known of a godly husband.

And Steve's love for Erik grew as well. While many men who father sons with severe disabilities spend their lifetimes mourning the fact that their sons will never play football, ride a bicycle, or become president, Steve became that rare exception who accepted and loved his son without conditions. Steve's love for Erik was never forced or faked. I never had the feeling that he loved Erik simply because he "had" to. As his relationship with the Lord matured, Steve began to love Erik just as our Father in heaven loves each of us: extravagantly and unreservedly.

Yes, Steve's life was radically changed by his acceptance of Jesus as his Lord and Savior. His life was characterized even more than before by kindness, generosity, and compassion. He was devoted to Lisa and Erik. He was a godly witness in his workplace. He served unselfishly in his church. In every aspect of his life, those incredible traits that defined his character before knowing the Lord became magnified and seemed to grow without confines. In every aspect of his life, he glorified the Lord Jesus Christ. And on Easter Sunday, just a few months after being baptized, he was called home to his heavenly Father. Steve was forty-three years old.

Lisa took Steve to the hospital at eight o'clock in the morning. At two o'clock in the afternoon she was sitting in the family room of the hospital, all alone, railing against God for taking her husband from her. She was angry, oh so very angry! Strong words flew from her mouth without reservation.

"God, I don't get it! I don't get *You!* How could you allow this to happen? What are You doing? Don't You care?"

Then she suddenly raised her head, and in the midst of that heart-wrenching anger, she had a vision of Steve striding confidently toward the exit doors of the hospital, a contented, even joyous, smile on his face. She knew where he was headed, and in the midst of her overwhelming anger, Lisa was given the blessing of peace, the perfect peace that comes only from the goodness of our God and Father.

While loss of such devastating proportions is not something we celebrate, the fact that we can share such vehement and bitter anger with our Lord is. Lisa learned right then and there that we must not be afraid to share our rage with God. He desires a most intimate relationship with each of us, and that includes not only reveling in our praise, but listening closely to our anger. And He is the only one who can transform that anger into thankfulness and peace, the only one who can create celebration out of sadness.

Though overwhelmed with loss and grief, Lisa was reminded of her faith in Jesus' promises. She knew her separation from Steve was only temporary. She was confident that one day her loving Lord would wipe away all tears from her eyes and she would be reunited with Steve, never to be parted again.

Steve left this earth for a heavenly mansion largely because a ministry was in place to meet the unique needs of his family. How grateful I am to have been a part of that ministry! When our staff and volunteers put hands and hearts to the love of Christ, they gave Steve a gift even more precious than the respite care or support groups or camps or Sunday school programs they provided for his son—they gave Steve the precious gift of eternal life.

That same disability ministry, and the body of believers it is a part of, continues to stand equipped and ready to provide the comfort and reassurance Lisa needs to make it through the dark days that still appear every now and again. It has been seventeen years since the Lord called Steve home, and Lisa is able to face depression and grief, confident that her Lord will deliver her from heartache and despair—confident that in His perfect time, He will deliver her, victorious, to her heavenly home where, one day, she and Steve will celebrate Erik as he stands in the glorious presence of His creator, whole and complete.

In my life, Erik, with his ear-to-ear grin and infectious laugh, has been one of God's angelic messengers. He is one of our Lord's most eloquent spokesmen! At a time in my life when I was hungering desperately for the reassurance that God had not forgotten or forsaken me, Erik comforted me in his own incomparable style. After not having seen him for over two years, I wondered if he would even know me. As I lifted Erik from his wheelchair for a hug, his eyes were glued to mine and his hands explored the once-familiar contours of my face. He was "in my face," and the delight that radiated from his toothy smile assured me that *he knew me*. Later that night, I couldn't get the incident out of my mind, and suddenly it struck me—*HE knows me!* Just as Erik had not forgotten me, neither had my Lord. No matter how far away I might have felt, the love of Christ was indeed constant and ever-present. My Father in heaven, who numbers the very hairs on my head, will never forsake or forget me. It was with a grateful heart that I prayed that night, thankful for this very special "hallelujah moment" that reminded me of the never-failing faithfulness of God's love.

I am so thankful for all the "hallelujah moments" my Lord has blessed me with through this precious little family, moments that serve as poignant reminders that in the midst of chaos and tragedy, there is indeed cause for celebration. God is walking through the valley with us, and in His time, He will take from us our anger, our grief, even our feelings of separation, and will restore us to Himself in peace.

Another Step Further

1. Read Psalm 32 in its entirety. What touched your heart in this psalm?

   _____

   _____

   _____

2. Are you celebrating and singing, "raising the roof," with your praise? Why or why not?

   _____

   _____

   _____

3. What do you have to celebrate? Grab a pencil and make a list. Wow! You really do have reasons to sing and raise the roof, don't you? Take a moment just now to go through your list, item by item, thanking the Lord for His grace and generosity.

   _____

   _____

   _____

4. Review your list again. Choose one person who comes to mind as you ponder the reasons you have to celebrate and take a few moments to write down how blessed you are by his or her presence in your life. Now pick up the phone, write an e-mail, or, better yet, write a note in your own hand and send it through the mail the good old-fashioned way to this special person. Your kindness may be just the thing to lift a weary heart and prompt them to consider all he or she has to celebrate as well.

_____

_____

_____

5. Read Psalm 88. Have you ever been that angry with God? Did you allow yourself to voice that anger? If not, allow yourself to do so now on the lines below. Your cries will reach His ears and His heart, and He will move heaven and earth to embrace you with His love and enfold you in His peace.

_____

_____

_____

Chapter Two

Fear Not

Don't be afraid for I am with you. Don't be discouraged, for I am your God. I will strengthen you and help you. I will hold you up with my victorious right hand.

—Isaiah 41:10 (NLT)

In Satan's arsenal of weapons, fear is probably his most effective. And why is that? Because it paralyzes us, it leaves us cowering in the corner, totally incapacitated. And the enemy is pleased indeed when he reduces us to silence and immobility because in that state we can't possibly proclaim the glory of God or share the hope of Jesus or minister to those in need. Yes, indeed, fear is a favorite of Satan's tactics, and he knows how to milk it for all it's worth.

In the summer of 1987, I journeyed to Zambia, Africa. I went to spend six weeks with my dear friends, John and Gail Douglas, who were serving as missionaries with Zambia Christian Mission. While they lived in the small town of Chipata, their work was in villages (many of them quite a ways out in the bush) where they established churches, trained leaders, and nurtured the body of Christ. I was blessed to have many opportunities to work with the women and children in these villages, one of which was nearly a day's journey away and very remote.

As we made the long journey to this particular village, John and Gail told stories about the village and its inhabitants—stories that included the fact that oftentimes people who were wandering around late at night (or even sometimes in the daylight!) were carried off by hungry lions. Well, when we finally arrived at our destination, it was definitely out in the bush! Camp was set up as John pitched a very large tent. The expectation was that all of us—the Douglas family, me, interns—would sleep in this humongous tent. I took one look at it and said as sweetly as possible, "No way!" All I could think of was the veritable zoo of slithery, slimy, decidedly unpleasant reptiles that might take a fancy to snuggling with me in my sleeping bag as I slept on the floor of that tent. I pleaded to be able to sleep in the back of the truck under the camper shell, and while I endured no end to teasing because of my cowardice, it was agreed that the back of the truck would serve as my sleeping chamber.

That night when everyone else went to snooze in the tent, I crawled into the back of the truck, which was parked some distance away. As I lay there, gazing out of the window at what seemed to be a gazillion brilliant stars, sleeping alone all of a sudden didn't seem like such a great idea. I was lying there listening to the drums beating (it was Africa, after all!) and the sounds of singing in a language I didn't understand. Even though I knew it was the village Christians who were singing, I was still scared half to death . . . suddenly realizing how far away I was from my home, *and* from my friends in the tent! Cartoon visions of folks suspended in giant cooking pots over a roaring fire came to mind. Silly, of course, but when I heard some rustling in the grass and a distant roar, the story of the villagers being carried away by hungry lions came to mind as well, and that was it. I was paralyzed with fear. All I could think of was some giant starving feline dragging me out of the back of the truck (pretty silly since I don't think lions can open latches!) and making me his dinner.

All night I lay there praying, "Please, God, don't let me have to go to the bathroom until it's light!" because I was sure if I had to journey the few hundred yards to the outhouse, I would become some furry animal's blue plate special en route. Instead of lying there and praising our Lord and Savior for the glory of His creation and for the way He had brought me to this marvelous place, I was fretting and worrying about becoming some critter's midnight snack! And that night I spent not sleeping because I allowed fear to reign, sapped my energy and I'm certain affected my ministry and effectiveness. The enemy had met me at my fear and used it to his advantage.

And that's how he works, isn't it? He gets us when we are most vulnerable, which is very often when we are afraid, and he uses that fear to render us incapable of praising or serving or glorifying God. Satan roars like a full-grown, predatory lion, right in our ears—threatening, accusing, seeking to destroy; but we need not fear! Jesus stands ready to defend us, to protect us, and to lead us through the barrage of fiery darts the enemy shoots our way as he seeks to gain a foothold in our lives and hearts.

In my computer room at home, I have a photograph of a lion that I took as he crossed the road about eight feet from the back of the truck I was riding in during a visit to the South Luangwa National Park while in Zambia. He looks harmless enough, focused as he was on rejoining his pride on the other side of the road, but I have to tell you he was an awesome sight and it wasn't without reservation that I snapped this picture. I keep this picture as a reminder of the fear I experienced that night in the back of the truck and how it left me vulnerable to the enemy's plan to thwart my effectiveness in ministry.

Lions are intimidating and dangerous animals, to say the least. It is very interesting to me that the enemy is likened to a lion in Scripture. Peter tells us, "Stay alert! Watch out for your great enemy, the devil. He prowls around like a roaring lion, looking for someone to devour" (1 Peter 5:8, NLT). Hm . . . this got me to thinking—it might be interesting to take a look at some of the characteristics of lions and see what we can learn about Satan's character at the same time.

First, lions are the only truly social cat species. They hunt and live as a team. Well, the enemy has a team, too. Ephesians 6:12 tells us, in part, that our struggle is "against the rulers, against the authorities, against the powers of this dark world and against the spiritual forces of evil . . ." (NIV). Satan has legions of dastardly cohorts ready and willing to do his bidding.

Second, an adult lion's roar can be heard up to five miles away. We all know from our own experience that the enemy's siren song is heard far and near. His devastating influence reaches every corner of the world.

Third, lions can "throw" their voices. Just as lions throw their voices to confuse their prey and cause chaos, so the enemy does with us. He makes his voice seem as if it comes from innocent and well-meaning sources ("Come on, it won't hurt if you have just one drink . . .") while all the while he is seeking to destroy us.

Fourth, lions can see well in the dark. The enemy loves the darkness, for it is there that he can be most effective. It is when our lives seem the most dark that we are the most vulnerable to his attack.

Fifth, lions rest and sleep during the day because it is nearly impossible to mount an attack in the daylight. When there is light, the light of Jesus, in our lives, all Satan can do is sit back and wait for darkness to descend. First John 1:5b tells us that "God is light, and in Him there is no darkness at all" (NIV). We must surround ourselves at all times with His light to protect ourselves from that hungry lion seeking to devour us.

Sixth, lions are particularly adept at locating moving objects. What is our tendency when darkness is upon us? We scatter and run as fast as we can. And while we dash all over the place, thinking we will evade the enemy's snare, we are really making it easier for him to catch us. So what is our best line of defense against an enemy that is so good at capturing moving targets?—to remain rooted and to stand firm in the light of Christ. First Corinthians 16:13a tells us to "be on your guard; stand firm in the faith" (NIV).

Last, rubbery pads on the feet of lions allow for a soft and noiseless tread. Lions depend on stealth to approach within close range of their prey. Satan is sneaky as well. He approaches without us even being aware of his presence, and before we know it, we are in his grasp. He uses stealth and cunning to corner us. And just like the lion, he expects to find a target that is completely unaware of his presence and unprepared to resist. That's why it is so important that we learn about these character traits of his—so we will not be unsuspecting victims, but rather, victorious soldiers against his schemes.

Through all these lion-like traits, Satan is able to instill fear in our hearts, and that fear is a real threat to our walk and to our ministry. Whether your fear is as silly as mine is of 7-Eleven markets or as serious as an overly compulsive fear of germs . . . no matter what the fear, the results are the same: when it rules our lives, it renders us useless to our Father's kingdom.

So, friends, let's follow the Lord's advice and "fear not." He's told us that literally hundreds of times in the Bible! Let's follow Jesus' example and muster the most powerful weapons we can against fear—Scripture and prayer. It's a "hallelujah moment" indeed when we realize that just as John told us, "perfect love casts out fear" and the love our Savior has for each of us is absolutely perfect.

Another Step Further

1. Read Matthew 4:1-11. How did Jesus resist the schemes of the devil and overcome fear at the beginning of His ministry?

   _____

   _____

   _____

2. How can you protect yourself with Scripture as Jesus did?

   _____

   _____

   _____

3. Read Matthew 26:36-44. What defensive method did Jesus use in the Garden of Gethsemane?

   _____

   _____

   _____

4. Give your fear, whatever it is, over to Jesus through prayer. Start with what you consider your most debilitating fear. Write it on a piece of paper. As you pray, asking Jesus to take this fear from you, crumple that paper as hard as you can or tear it into a zillion pieces. Destroying that paper is a visible representation of how the perfect love of Christ destroys the fear in our hearts. Doesn't that feel good?

_____

_____

_____

5. Now meditate on Proverbs 3:24-26 and praise God that you are never alone in your fear.

_____

_____

_____

Chapter Three

A Gridiron Analogy for Life

I'm not saying that I have this all together, that I have it made. But I am well on my way, reaching out for Christ, who has so wondrously reached out for me. Friends, don't get me wrong: By no means do I count myself an expert in all of this, but I've got my eye on the goal, where God is beckoning us onward—to Jesus. I'm off and running, and I'm not turning back. So let's keep focused on that goal, those of us who want everything God has for us. If any of you have something else in mind, something less than total commitment, God will clear your blurred vision—you'll see it yet! Now that we're on the right track, let's stay on it!

—Philippians 3:14-16 (MSG)

Jane Lynn Simmons

Football is a manly game to be sure, but it's a sport I am actually familiar with. From the time I was a very little girl, football was a big part of my life. My uncle Dick was sixteen when I was born, already a high school football standout; and by the time I was three, he was a star wide receiver for the Whittier College team. His home games were a family affair—my parents and grandparents would pack me up along with a picnic lunch, and off we'd go to spend the afternoon in the stadium. And always, when the game was over, we would go down on the field to congratulate, or console, as the case may be, my uncle and his teammates. I was a pint-sized mascot for the team, carried around the field on the shoulders of Uncle Dick's best friend, Paul Cheeves, affectionately referred to as "Cheese" by my little toddler self.

As I became school-age, my uncle began a career as a winning high school football coach, and by the time I was in graduate school, he was coaching at the University of Southern California. He eventually headed to the National Football League, first as director of operations for the Tampa

Bay Buccaneers and later in that same position with the Los Angeles Rams.

All those years, our family loved football and attended as many games as we could. As a child, I especially loved going to games with my grandparents when my uncle was a high school coach because they were so proud of him, and it didn't matter whether his team won or lost! I learned a valuable lesson about unconditional love in the venue of a high school football stadium, of all places, thanks to my dear grandparents. I learned a valuable lesson about gratitude there as well.

In November of 1960, while attending one of my uncle's games, the announcer asked for everyone in the stadium to rise for a moment of silence. Being only eight years old, I was not quite sure what this was all about, but the announcer explained that we were standing in silence to honor sixteen members of the Cal Poly San Luis Obispo football team, one equipment manager, one booster, and four others who had been killed just a few days before in a plane crash at the airport in Toledo, Ohio. Their plane had crashed and burned as they took off on what was supposed to be their return flight after playing Bowling Green State University. I saw tears in my grandfather's eyes as we stood, and that really got my attention. Knowing the gruff old guy that he was, I was unaccustomed to seeing such a blatant display of emotion. This tragedy had deeply touched him, and his usual stoicism was replaced by raw emotion.

I remember that later, on the long drive home after the game, he repeatedly expressed his sadness over this terrible event, his compassion for the Cal Poly families affected, and his fervent, intense gratitude for his family's safety. It wasn't until many years later that I realized my grandfather was teaching me that tragedies like this are not isolated events in the course of human history, but rather, they are happenings that should have a profound effect on us all, motivating us not only to compassion for the victims but also to a deeper appreciation and gratitude for the blessings in our own lives. I am very grateful that in his wisdom, my grandfather taught me, through his example, that when our lives are touched by heartbreaking events such as this, 1 Thessalonians 5:16-18 clearly defines what our response should be: "Be cheerful, no matter what; pray all the time; thank God no matter what happens. This is the way God wants you who belong to Christ Jesus to live" (MSG).

Several years ago, the women's ministry leader at the church I was attending asked if I would speak at a "Soup-er Sunday" ladies luncheon to take place around the time of the Super Bowl. She asked if I could share my testimony in a way that somehow related to football. After agreeing, I wondered how on earth that was possible . . . I mean, really, *football?* But, as I sat down at my computer to begin writing, the Holy Spirit lead the way, and I was utterly amazed at how easily my testimony fit into a gridiron analogy!

So let's start with what every football game starts with—preparation. With diligent zeal on the part of their coaches, players are prepared to meet their opponents. Coaches spend endless hours instructing their players, exercising their bodies and minds, preparing them to meet any situation they may face on the playing field with confidence and an effective strategy.

Well, my testimony begins with the preparation I received from my parents for the game of life. Just as football players are raised up, in a sense, by their coaches, I was raised up in a loving, stable Christian home where there were the usual family altercations ("You did *what* with my pink blouse?"), but where no one spoke in loud or harsh voices and where everyone was made to feel valued and special. My parents were quite strict about many things and, in fact, for several years, the only TV programs my sister and I were allowed to watch were *Lassie* and *The Wonderful World of Disney*, and the entire family, including our own mini-Lassie, watched those programs together.

My parents modeled Christlike behavior in many ways, instructing us faithfully in the ways of the Lord and raising us within the larger church family. Early on, we were taught the value of mercy, generosity, and service by their example. My parents were as diligent in my preparation for the game of life as any coach preparing his players for the "big" game.

After preparation for the game, but before the game actually begins, there are always pregame festivities. For a football game, the pregame festivities usually include various kinds of entertainment, all designed to get the adrenaline flowing so everyone is excited about what is to come. I would say my baptism was the pregame festivity for my Christian life. I was sixteen years old (oh, such a long time ago!), and I still remember distinctly how I felt: the unbridled enthusiasm, the feeling that now that I had confessed Jesus as my Lord and Savior I could be victorious—wait, not just victorious, but triumphant—in the game of life ahead of me. You know how riled up the fans are after pregame festivities, how certain they feel that their team will vanquish its foe? That's how I felt after my baptism; I was certain there wasn't an opponent in the world I couldn't rout.

But then I entered the game. I sailed through high school, happy as a clam, and began my journey through college and graduate school. A strange thing happened on my way to that master's degree though. Just as the University of California at Berkeley's Roy Riegels did during the Rose Bowl game of 1929, I began running in the wrong direction. I discovered partying and wine and boys and became obsessed with appearances (or more to the point, with shoes!). I was selfish, self-absorbed, and had made a drastic diversion from the original game plan. I had become a promiscuous party girl, and while I still excelled in my studies, I had become a rogue player, ignoring the advice of my "coaches" and playing the game to suit my own desire, which was to get out from under their influence and play solo, making my own money, spending it any way I liked, and living my life however I wanted. I was functioning like a "free agent," like my contract with the team of the brotherhood of Christ had expired and I was looking to sign with another franchise! The dark side was beckoning, none too subtly; my focus was not on *the* prize; and I was sliding headlong down the slippery slope of serial sin. You know those guys who sit in the stands at games with their faces and bodies painted outrageously, being obnoxious and taunting the players on the other team, trying to take their focus off the game? Well, the enemy and his cohorts were definitely playing that role in my life with great success by placing temptations in my path to which they knew I would be particularly susceptible.

I had become a rebellious, ungodly young woman!

Well, I completed graduate school, and with master's degree in hand, I accepted my first professional position. I moved as far away from home as possible and began playing my version of the game of life in earnest. The partying and promiscuity continued until one morning I woke up in a place I didn't remember going to, with a guy whose name I didn't know, and with a headache the likes of which I was certain was unprecedented in human experience. As I drove home, I suddenly realized that the only game I was in was one whose sole purpose was to end with my total self-destruction.

As I drove down a lonely stretch of Highway 395, I cried and prayed and begged for the Lord to show me what to do. I knew I had to get my life together, but I felt so lost, so far from not only my earthly family home but my heavenly home as well. I had isolated myself from my coaches and teammates, and suddenly that invincibility I felt as a free agent gave way to abject vulnerability. Much like a quarterback who suddenly finds himself facing a horde of defensive linemen twice his size without any protection from his teammates, I recognized the fact that I was about to be sacked, pulled under, and plowed over, and I desperately began hunting for a way out.

There was a gentleman I met with every month when I turned my attendance registers and therapy logs in to the county office of education. He somehow sensed this sudden emptiness in me, saw an opportunity, and seized it. He invited me to his church. That could have been a good thing, since getting back on the field with the family of God was exactly what I needed, but he was a member of a modern-day cult.

I was hurting. Pain clouded my rationality and rendered me deaf to the warnings and urgings of the Holy Spirit. Oh brother, here I was signing a contract with yet another team, having been drafted by some very clever agents. I spent two years in that church, and looking back on it now, I am astounded by the entire experience. All along, there was a nagging ache in my heart and I chose to ignore it because I was so needy. The enemy had made this answer to that need irresistibly attractive, and I became a real team player, immersing myself in the activities and doctrine of the church. For the longest time I allowed myself to be blissfully unaware of the fact that I had signed on with a team that was destined to ultimately lose.

I was choosing to ignore the Holy Spirit who had become a part of me when I accepted Christ Jesus as my Lord and Savior oh so long ago. You know how the refs in a football game call fouls and point out to offending players the error of their ways? Well, the Holy Spirit was about to call me for a personal foul and yank me from the game!

Through a series of what I see now as providential circumstances, I found myself being offered a position back home in southern California. Something (in hindsight I realize it was the pleadings of the Holy Spirit) told me I needed to go home—both literally and figuratively. So I accepted the position offered to me in a middle school. Seriously? Middle school? Our precious Lord's use of this position was a sure sign of His perfect sense of humor (and a valuable lesson in His sovereignty) since I had adamantly vowed I would *never* teach junior high schoolers!

Well, not only did the Lord lead me home, but He put me in the direct path of scouts from the winning team! After a blessedly brief stint at the middle school, I was given the opportunity to transfer to an elementary school. Imagine my surprise when my new instructional assistant showed up and I discovered her husband was the pastor of a local church from the same brotherhood of Christian churches as I had grown up in! Immediately she invited me to visit on Sunday morning, and immediately I found one excuse after another not to do so. I weakly tried to claim I already belonged to a church, I claimed family obligations, I feigned illness, but finally, the call of the truth became so strong I could no longer ignore it.

I agreed to visit Crossroads Christian Church in Corona one Sunday, and lo and behold, the second I walked through the doors I felt much like what I think a football player must feel like when he runs onto the field in his home stadium filled with fans—I could almost hear the angels cheering from the rafters, "Hallelujah, victory is at hand!"

I found myself surrounded by coaches and teammates, brothers and sisters in the Lord who, whether they knew it or not, were calling me from the despair of the sidelines to get back into the game.

The Christlike coaching of my new church family, teamed with the long-suffering but never failing love and prayers of my family, got me back into the game. My days of running lickety-split toward the wrong goal were over . . . or so I thought!

As any parent of a child who participates in sports knows, when kids are in the heat of the game, injuries are inevitable. When you put yourself in the middle of the fray, you are bound to get beat up in some fashion because what opponent is ever going to go down without a fight?

As I became involved in Bible studies and a variety of ministries during my first year or two at my new church home, I felt such peace, such a blessed connection and camaraderie with my "teammates," such a deep and abiding relationship with Jesus, I simply could not imagine ever allowing myself to again become a "free agent" playing for the opposition.

But the enemy and his team are clever opponents, and they have their own game plan that is deviously based on our weaknesses. When they do tackle us, they hit us hard and they hit us fast in the areas where we are most vulnerable. They take us down with the intent of keeping us from ever reaching the end zone and God's ultimate goal for us.

Sure enough, I let the influences of the opposing team into my life once more . . . suddenly there was a man in my life, and I was faced with the conflict of desire versus righteousness. Thus began a gradual backslide. Like the player who has the ball and is in a position to run all the way to the end zone for a touchdown, but fumbles, I found myself fumbling . . . big time! But this time, the fumbling did not come without guilt and a constant awareness of how that fumbling must have been grieving my Lord. Thank goodness for that!

This time, instead of just becoming a rogue free agent and living a "looking for Mr. Goodbar" lifestyle, I acknowledged my fumbling to Jesus and cried and prayed fervently for Him to show me my value in His eyes. I begged Him to help me see, deep in my heart and soul, that how He saw me was all that mattered and that my relationship with Him as my Lord and Savior was *the* most important relationship in my life, that any other relationship that drew my focus away from Him and toward behavior unacceptable in His eyes was simply not okay. I wanted so much for Jesus to reveal His purpose for my life. And all the while, despite crying out to Jesus in a state of utter brokenness, I was becoming weaker and fumbling more and more with each passing day.

But what does Scripture tell us happens when we are persistent in our crying out? When we cry out with a sincere heart? Psalm 34:17 tells us, "The Lord hears His people when they call to Him for help. He rescues them from their troubles" (NLT). We are assured our Father in heaven will answer—and He did indeed answer me in a way I just could not ignore.

As those who know me well would tell you, I am a creature of habit. Okay, well, maybe it's more extreme than that, but be that as it may, one of the things I rarely vary in my life is the route I take driving to or from work, to or from church, to or from the grocery store, to and from my friends' homes . . . well, you get the picture. At this time in my life I had a particular route I drove home from the school where I was a special day class teacher for communicatively handicapped students—I had the route between those two places timed with precision. I never varied from this route, and I could tell you exactly how many minutes it was between various landmarks on my journey home.

One day as I got in my car to head homeward, I felt the urging to take a different route home. As I put the car in gear and headed for the freeway, this urge became an overwhelming impulse. I took the alternate route. Midway through my journey homeward, what is known in California as a "Sig alert" was broadcast on the radio. (A Sig alert is defined by the California Highway Patrol as any unplanned event that causes the closing of one lane of traffic for thirty minutes or more.) The alert being described by the radio announcer involved a horrendous multicar accident with numerous critical injuries and fatalities. I realized with shocking clarity that this tragedy had taken place on my usual route home at exactly the time I would have been in that area.

How do I describe the acute sense of divine intervention that flooded my soul? In that very moment I understood. My precious Lord had answered my prayers in a way I absolutely could not deny or ignore—He had saved me from injury, perhaps even death. How could I doubt that He had a purpose for my life? How could I deny His love for me? How could I willingly choose to serve the world when He most assuredly had set me apart to serve His kingdom? I could not. My heart was full to overflowing as I praised and thanked Him for His glorious intervention in my life and His clear, undeniable answer to my prayers. As I got out of my car after arriving safely at home, I was filled with eager anticipation for what He had in store for me. I knew beyond a shadow of a doubt that He had preserved me for a purpose, and I was anxious to find out what that purpose was! Just like the freshman who can't quite believe he has made the varsity team, I was looking forward to seeing exactly how the Lord planned to use me.

The answer to that question came in very short order! That very same week, I was asked to teach a Sunday school class for young adults with developmental disabilities. The class was started by Sharon Elkins, the precious mom of a young man with Down syndrome, and she and a small group of volunteers had faithfully served as teachers in this class of five students for a couple of years.

But the time had come for these folks to move on to other areas of ministry. I was approached to become the teacher because special education was my profession. I pointed out that I was a special day class teacher for very young students who were speech and language impaired. I had never worked with young adults with developmental disabilities. I was not feeling up to the challenge, but how could I deny any service asked of me by the Lord when just a couple of days before He had saved my life? Perhaps this little class and these students were the key to His purpose for my life. I was doubtful, but willing to give it a try. Just like the aspiring football player who has always pictured himself as a quarterback but is asked to be the place kicker, I had to trust the Lord (as the player trusts his coach) and believe with all my heart that He was leading me on the right track.

So, despite my insecurity, I began as the teacher of the Chosen Ones Sunday school class. The first day I taught there were the usual five students in the class. They eyed me with some trepidation at first and rightly so. They were quick to inform me that the lesson I had planned was too short, the craft activity too complicated, I did not know how to conduct the prayer circle the right way, and I brought baby snacks! Yikes! They all wanted to know where their *real* teacher was. When the students had all left the classroom, I put my head down on one of the tables and dejectedly muttered, "Oh, dear Lord, what have you gotten me into?"

Who could have guessed what would transpire just two Sundays later? Refreshed and renewed after a week of intense prayer, I came to class better prepared and anxious to forge ahead the second week. And lo and behold, by the third week, we had not five students, but eighteen! And not only that, all the previous volunteers had been replaced *twice over* by competent, godly men and women with true servant's hearts! To my great amazement, the class and the volunteer base had more than tripled in just two weeks' time! I began to sense that the Lord had some pretty big plans in mind for us, and by my second month in the class, I knew without a doubt that something was up because our class had nearly doubled again—there were now thirty-one students—and even more incredible people had come forward to volunteer! Only the

Lord Himself could have engineered such growth. With the increased number of students came an increased awareness of needs, and a full-fledged disability ministry was born from the seed of that tiny little Sunday school class. Like the podunk athletic program that gives rise to a Cinderella team that wins the national title, our Chosen Ones class was the genesis for one of the first and most comprehensive ministries in our country designed specifically to meet the needs of families experiencing disability.

And for me, glory be! I had my very own cheerleaders! They may not have been as coordinated or as gorgeous in the world's eyes as the cheerleaders we see on TV urging their teams to victory, but they were no less enthusiastic. These cheerleaders of mine, the many persons with disabilities that God graced my life with, touched my heart in ways no one else on earth had ever done. It was these cheerleaders, and their dear families, who finally drew me into a relationship of *complete* trust and dependence on the Lord Jesus. They taught me not only how to love in purity but, even more importantly, they taught me how to accept pure love. My dear friends whom the world considers "disabled" were the only ones who got me turned around and headed back toward the right end zone and the goal Jesus had set before me!

As you are probably aware, there is a great deal of security in place during professional football games. No effort or expense is spared in keeping the thousands of people who fill the stadiums safe. Well, we have even better security for our game of life. The Holy Spirit indwells us with our very own built-in security system *and* we have the gift of God's Word that includes everything we need to keep us safe from anyone or anything that desires to harm us. Quarterbacks on a football field who find themselves all alone are bound to get sacked by their opponents; but we, as children of God, are never alone. And even when the players of the opposing team, the enemy and his cohorts, are in hot pursuit, we are protected.

But despite that protection, our opponents never throw in the towel, do they? They are always on the lookout for a hole in our defensive line. If they can't tackle us one way, they'll find another. That certainly has been true in my life. I may have been first and goal with victory in sight having routed sexual temptation and remaining strong in my resolve, but that wily opponent came at me with a tackle of a different sort . . . I found myself in the hospital, having a hysterectomy at a very young age and facing the enemy on a playing field far different than I had ever expected.

All my life I had wanted to be a mom. I was crushed when that privilege was taken from me so abruptly. And while this was just something that happened in my body, the way I perceived it and reacted to it turned it into the devil's playing field. I was so mad! I was lying wounded on the playing field, and while the opposing team would have loved to see me flounder there all alone, I was quickly ministered to by my teammates and cheerleaders, and just like an injured football player is carried off the field on a stretcher surrounded by people dedicated to his well-being, so I was carried from overwhelming depression and anger to a renewed sense of commitment to Jesus and to disability ministry. I may not have won the prize of motherhood, but I became acutely aware of the fact that the championship belonged to my team and that the ultimate victory had already been won on our behalf!

During the years that have passed since then, I have become very aware of the fact that the opposing team members never leave the stadium with their tails between their legs and their heads bowed down in defeat—nope; they never give up their efforts to win you to their side! Through the circumstances we face in the game of life, the enemy and his team seeks relentlessly for our vulnerability and tries to defeat us by negatively influencing our reactions to those circumstances. But, if we listen to our head coach, the Holy Spirit, we can face those circumstances with the joy of the Lord and the confidence that He will work everything for our good and for the good of His kingdom.

As I sit and write this, this year's football season is about to end with the Super Bowl. But our seasons of life continue—we will play games that we win and we will play games that we lose, but we can press on with the confidence that at the end of our season of life, through the love and sacrifice of our Lord Jesus, the ultimate victory will be ours.

And what is that victory? Its eternity spent in heaven, of course. We "press on," as Paul writes, toward the goal that sits gloriously in the end zone of heaven—life eternal in the presence of our Lord and Savior and our loving, faithful Creator.

I'm not perfect—far from it—but by golly, now that I've surpassed the halftime of my game of life, I know for certain whose team I'm on—and it's the one that will always win in the end! Dear friends, I am here to tell you that we have a coach who never gives up on us, who never leaves us to play the game alone. And despite how many times we may run in the wrong direction, fumble the ball, or divert from His game plan for a time, He is always there. And He has a great cloud of witnesses cheering for us as we fight to the goal He has set before us. But even better than that, He has the postgame celebration already planned, and that "hallelujah moment" is going to last for eternity!

Another Step Further

1. Who are your coaches in the game of life? Who are your most ardent cheerleaders? Take time today to write them a note or call them and thank them for their guidance, support, and encouragement.

   _____
   _____
   _____

2. Ask the Lord if He might have someone for whom you can be a coach or cheerleader. When the Lord places that particular person on your heart, embrace your role with faithfulness and unconditional love. Be transparent. Keep a journal of how you, and the brother or sister you are mentoring, are able to reflect the power and grace of our Lord Jesus as you race toward the finish line of your earthly journey.

   _____
   _____
   _____

3. Hebrews 12:1-2 tells us in part, "And let us run with endurance the race God has set before us. We do this by keeping our eyes on Jesus . . ." (NLT). What particular obstacles has the enemy placed before you that try your patience and threaten to cause you to stumble as you strive for the prize? How can keeping your eyes on Jesus keep you on the path toward victory? What can you do to narrow your focus and avoid the worldly distractions that can sabotage your race?

_____

_____

_____

4. Runners have special equipment such as specially designed shoes, aerodynamic clothing, and a nutrient-rich diet that help them get the most out of their efforts. What "equipment" do you have at your disposal to enhance your ability to run the race of life with courage and stamina?

_____

_____

_____

5. What is your favorite sport? How can that sport be an analogy for your game of life?

   _____
   _____
   _____

Chapter Four

Shamed by the Weak

Take a good look, friends, at who you were when you got called into this life. I don't see many of the 'brightest and the best' among you, not many influential, not many from high society families. Isn't it obvious that God deliberately chose men and women that the culture overlooks and exploits and abuses, chose these 'nobodies' to expose the hollow pretensions of the 'somebodies'? That makes it quite clear that none of you can get by with blowing your own horn before God. Everything that we have—right thinking and right living, a clean slate and a fresh start—comes from God by way of Jesus Christ. That's why we have the saying, "If you're going to blow a horn, blow a trumpet for God."

—1 Corinthians 1:26-31 (MSG)

Jane Lynn Simmons

People have often asked me the "how and why" of my involvement in disability ministry and my choice of a career in special education. I think they expect to hear a heartrending story about a family member having a disability, or about having to deal with disability in my own life. But I don't have any stories like that. I have not had to experience disability on such a personal level until quite recently. My answer has always been that I have been involved in disability ministry and have chosen this particular career path simply because it was God's will for my life.

It all began many years ago when, as mentioned in the preceding chapter, I was asked to take over the teaching responsibilities in a Sunday school class of five young adults with developmental disabilities. When asked if I would accept this position, I thought, *I can handle this! I have a master's degree, for goodness sake, and I'm a special education teacher! How hard can it be?* Oh yes, dear friends, can you tell that a much-needed and invaluable lesson in humility was on its way?

As I wrote before, on the very first Sunday after all the students had left, I put my head down on the table and sighed ever so deeply as I thought, *Oh, my dear Lord, what have you gotten me into?* I could not believe I had committed a whole year of my life to teaching this class, and this first day had not been fun at all. In fact, it had been an unmitigated disaster! Everything that could go wrong had gone wrong that morning: the lesson was too short, the craft was too complicated, and the students all wanted to know (asking repeatedly, I might add) where their *real* teacher was. I was miserable!

But by the next Sunday, after much prayer by me and for me, I was refreshed and renewed. Things really went a lot better. The students had resigned themselves to my presence, and I began to sense from them a very special kind of love—genuine and unconditional. *Well, maybe this won't be so bad after all,* I thought after that second Sunday. Little did I know that the Lord was working in a mighty way to dramatically change my life and the lives of many families experiencing disability.

Then, amazingly, on my third Sunday, I arrived to discover our class had more than tripled in size!!! Here were eighteen eager students, all with some form of developmental disability, and I began to sense that our precious Lord was preparing our church family for an incredible work. I could never have dreamed what He had in store for our church body, for our students with disabilities and their families, or for me personally. I could not have imagined what the extent of the ministry branching out from this small Sunday school class would be or that within a few short years it would be involved in the lives of more than one hundred families experiencing disability.

Dear friends, I want you to know that I am the person I am today because of the impact that these folks with disabilities and their families have had on my life. Who I am is a direct result of what I have learned from them. I have learned more about patience, about being content in whatever circumstances, about perseverance, and most importantly, about love that is constant and unconditional, from these precious folks than I ever could have learned from any other source. My friends with disabilities and their families have taught me important lessons about our God whom they love so deeply and proclaim so boldly. Their faith is so strong, so unwavering, yet so uncomplicated. Their belief in the Lord Jesus and in His ability to provide all they need is unshakeable. No wonder Jesus told us that we should all strive for faith that simple and that genuine.

In one of Disney's animated films, *The Hunchback of Notre Dame*[1] an interesting question is posed: "Who is the monster and who is a man?" One who is not familiar with the story might be tempted to agree with the answer of the antagonist, Frollo, who considers himself a man superior to Quasimodo, whom he considers to be a monster. But, as the story unfolds, the audience comes to realize that despite Quasimodo's deformities, his gentleness, selfless devotion, and nobility of character make him a man worthy of respect and dignity while Frollo's evil nature is truly monstrous.

This reminds me that in God's economy, value and worth are not based on beauty, wit, or productivity, but rather on the condition of the

---

[1] Directed by Gary Trousdale and Kirk Wise, produced by Don Hahn, distributed by Walt Disney Pictures and Buena Vista Distribution, released June 21, 1966.

heart. Because of the purity and sincerity of their hearts, God often uses those with disabilities to teach valuable lessons. Many times during my years in disability ministry Paul's words in 1 Corinthians 1:26-31 have been proven to me.

On the bulletin board in my office, I have a note that was passed down to me in church one Sunday many years ago. It is written on the back of a prayer card that has become tattered and frayed. The writing has begun to fade, but I have kept that note, and always will, because it reminds me of one of the kindest and most gracious persons I have ever known. The note reads: "Jane cry. Jesus make her happy. I worry you. Love, Shelly." Shelly had sensitively noticed that I was upset that morning and wrote that note to encourage me.

My friend Shelly is quite a gal! If you had visited the church she and I attended together, you would have seen her during the first service sitting on the front pew right next to the pastor. She would give him an encouraging pat on the back as he got up to preach and then, depending on how she thought the sermon went, she would give him a hug or merely shake his hand as he sat down again.

During the second service she led music in her disabilities ministry Sunday school class that had upwards of thirty members. Then finally, during the third service, she could be found volunteering in a toddler Sunday school class.

Yes, Shelly is one remarkable woman! her favorite movie is *Grease;* she loves to eat chili fries, and she has Down syndrome. Despite her very apparent disability, Shelly's wisdom in the ways of the Lord, her boundless love for Him, and her desire to tirelessly serve Him have led me through the years to a deeper commitment to the Lord Jesus Christ. Shelly's ministrations of kindness and gentleness have often humbled and convicted me. Whenever someone in her Sunday school class had a birthday or was sick, there was a card from Shelly. When one of our disability ministry volunteers got married or had a baby, there was a gift from Shelly. Shelly says she'll pray for you and she does it. She is quick to intercede and slow to give up, and because of her sweet, yet persistent ways, she is a convincing witness. Many of her friends have come to a saving knowledge of Christ because of her one-woman evangelistic campaign.

I have been the recipient of Shelly's kindness on many occasions, but the one I remember best occurred when she was hospitalized with a brand-new diagnosis of lupus, a disease that can be a deadly combination with Down syndrome. I had visited her in the hospital every day after school for a week, and by Friday evening I was exhausted. After we had talked for just a brief minute or two, Shelly took my hand and said, "Jane, go home! You tired." I began to weep. In a mere second I had been humbled by my dear friend's selflessness. I hate to admit it, but had I been the person in that hospital bed, facing a life-threatening situation, I wouldn't have been about to let a visitor go, no matter how tired he or she was! Very selfishly, I would have clung to anyone who came to see me. But not Shelly—she gently prodded me to go home until I finally gave in. I learned firsthand from Shelly that loving kindness is not selfish or self-centered; rather, it always puts others first.

As I think about my dear friend Shelly, I am reminded of a particular incident that occurred the first night of a weeklong camping adventure. After church one Sunday, Shelly and I, along with five other young ladies with developmental disabilities, made a long journey by car into the mountains and hiked for nearly an hour to the teepee that would be our home for the next several days. After a busy afternoon and evening we were finally settled in and ready for some much-needed sleep, but we had a problem. A big problem! One of my campers was frightened and would not turn off her flashlight—and it wasn't a regular-sized flashlight, it was gigantic! The light was disturbing everyone in our teepee as well as our neighbors!

I tried without success to convince this young woman that everything was fine, that I wouldn't let anything happen to her, that she really would be safe and sound even if she turned the light off. I cajoled, I bribed, I reasoned, all to no avail. As my patience reached the breaking point and I began to get angry, Shelly's strong voice entered the fray. From her cot, she asked her friend if she remembered what we had talked about in Sunday school that morning. (I couldn't even remember at that point!) When she replied that she didn't remember, Shelly gently but firmly reminded her that the lesson had been about Jesus and the fact that He is with us no matter where we are. "Do you believe that?" Shelley asked. "Yes," her friend replied. "Then, if Jesus is here in our teepee, you can turn off your flashlight." Who could argue with faith like that? In amazement, I thanked the Lord as the light went out. The issue was never raised again.

How humbled I was by Shelly's wisdom and by her ability to handle a difficult situation with such grace and maturity. I quietly praised our God and Father for the blessing of seeing the unquestionable meaning of Paul's words in 1 Corinthians 1:26-31 that night.

As long as persons with disabilities are not included in the full life of the church, as long as they are allowed to worship but not to fellowship or serve, our appreciation of the words of Paul remains piteously limited. God has created each of us with a unique purpose for our lives. We each have a job to do for the good of His kingdom and for the glory of our Lord Jesus Christ. Despite our abilities or disabilities, in the "hallelujah moments" of our lives God uses each of us in amazing ways to accomplish His purposes. Now, the question remains, are we willing to honor the ways in which He uses those whom the world might consider "weak," "foolish," "the least," or "poor?" As the body of Christ, we are called to do nothing less.

Another Step Further

1. Read Matthew 25:31-46.

   _____

   _____

   _____

2. Now read Galatians 4:12-14.

   _____

   _____

   _____

3. What do these passages tell you about how you should treat those who are considered by the world to be different, unlovable, unworthy, the least?

   _____

   _____

   _____

4. Is loving, accepting, and welcoming these folks optional? What will be the consequence of not including those with disabilities in the full life of the church?

_____

_____

_____

5. Read 2 Corinthians 12:9-10. Paul tells us that we are made strong in weakness, not because the weakness itself it glorified but because Christ is glorified through His power to use that weakness for good. Take a few minutes to reflect on this truth. Now ask our gracious Lord to reveal to you how He can use you in your weakest condition to bring glory to Himself and good to His kingdom.

_____

_____

_____

Chapter Five

Rejoice

Always be full of joy in the Lord. I say it again—rejoice!

—Philippians 4:4 (NLT)

Oh my goodness! There are so many things in life that bring us joy! Spending time with family and friends, a child's laughter and delight on Christmas morning, hugs, kisses, the glory of nature, the awesome wonder in the realization that you are loved by the Creator of the universe . . . the list could go on and on. In such circumstances, it's easy to be joyful, isn't it? Ah, but Paul wrote these words to remind us that joy is a reflection of our inner contentment and peace and not necessarily a reflection of what might be going on in our outward lives. He wrote those words from prison, for heaven's sake! There is nothing joyful about being in chains, and yet

Paul's heart was obviously overflowing with the joy of the Lord. How is it possible to rejoice in such a predicament? Because despite the trauma, the discouragement, and the pain of whatever we are called upon to endure, like Paul, we can indeed rejoice when we acknowledge and celebrate the fact that we are not alone, that our Lord and Savior Jesus Christ is by our side and will never leave us alone to face the trials of daily life.

One of the women I have learned much from in the Old Testament is Hannah. Hannah was the favorite and most beloved wife of Elkanah, but Hannah had a problem. She wanted to have children but could not conceive. Today, when a woman experiences what Hannah did, it is tragic to be sure; but in Hannah's day, when women found their identity only from being someone's wife and by having that man's children, Hannah's situation left her perceived as a woman with absolutely no purpose in life.

Hannah's barrenness was made even more painful because she was one of two wives, and the other wife, Peninah, had no problem at all producing children. Scripture tells us, in fact, that she had many children and that she ridiculed and tormented Hannah because she did not. My heart goes out to Hannah; every year on the annual trek to Shiloh for the holy days, there she would be—trudging along with Peninah making fun of her behind her back and with Peninah's kids constantly underfoot, reminding Hannah every step of the way of her inadequacies. It's no wonder that when they finally arrived in Shiloh, Hannah beat it for the temple posthaste to seek her Lord.

In the temple, Hannah cried out to God's heart as she laid bare her own breaking heart before Him. Hannah pleaded with God to give her a child, promising she would give the child back to Him as His servant if only she could conceive. God heard her cry. He blessed her with a son, Samuel. And Hannah kept her end of the bargain, which had to be incredibly difficult. When he was only three years old, she took Samuel to live at the temple to train for God's service. Can you imagine that? Leaving your tiny son permanently in the care of someone else at that tender age? But Hannah was a woman of integrity, and despite how that must have hurt, she kept her word. Samuel grew up to be one of the most important prophets and leaders in the Old Testament, and Hannah, through the pain of her sacrifice, found joy in the answer to her prayer.

We see from Hannah's life that when we cry out to our Lord, He will answer. He will meet us at our brokenness and honor our cries with His mercy, blessing, and favor—and through His answer, though it may not always be the desire of our heart, we can find contentment and joy.

I have learned much from Hannah's example because I can relate to her. I have had my own time of crying out to the Lord because I wanted a child. Having a hysterectomy at a young age did not dampen the passionate desire in my heart to be a mom. While doing some consulting work in a Russian orphanage, I found my sweet little Alexandra. She was eighteen months old and had Down syndrome—and I'm pretty sure we fell in love with each other at first hug. When I returned to the United States, after much prayer, I decided to adopt Alexandra, and from that point on for the next two and a half years, life became a roller coaster of hope and despair. Everything, literally everything, went along quickly and smoothly until it came time for the final approval of her departure that had to come from the woman who was in charge of adoptions in Moscow. Suddenly, it was like the whole process had hit an impenetrable wall. After fighting for Alexandra for over two years, I can remember sitting in the rocking chair in her room that was ready and waiting for her, clutching a quilt my mother had made for her, and crying out to Jesus for His mercy in this situation. I begged Him, "Please, Lord, do something."

A few days later I received a phone call with the news that Alexandra had died. As I drove home from work that evening in a haze of grief, I again called out to Jesus. This time, I was begging Him to quiet the enemy who was filling my heart and mind with his accusations. There had been a time in my past when I was not a very nice person and when habitual sin, partying, and promiscuity had me living a life that did not honor my Lord. The enemy chose this particular time after I received this devastating news, this time when I so vulnerable, to remind me of all the stupid and disgusting and immoral things I had once done—it was like he was right in my ear telling me that because I was such an awful person, I wasn't good enough to be a mom, that I didn't deserve to have a child.

I'm certain you can imagine how I cried out to Jesus during that drive home—recognizing that the enemy was making a play for my walk . . . and believe me, he was fighting dirty. But just as the Lord answered Hannah, He answered my cries as well. While I had never before nor have ever since felt as if I audibly heard His voice, I know without a doubt that at that moment in time I did. In the midst of the enemy's accusations, in the depth of my despair, His still, small voice clearly said, "She'll know you in heaven." Never have I heard more comforting words. While the pain of Alexandra's loss has been overwhelming at times, the hope of an eternity spent with her in the presence of the King sustains me and fills my heart with a joy so incredible it takes my breath away.

Yes, rejoicing is not just for the happy times of life. The rejoicing of "hallelujah moments" comes even more powerfully in those times of darkness and despair when nothing but the touch and voice of our ever-present and ever-loving Lord and Savior gives us hope for the future and the strength to journey on in the midst of our pain.

Another Step Further

1. Read 2 Corinthians 4:17-18 and Psalm 126:5.

   _____
   _____
   _____

2. What events or circumstances in your life have robbed you of your joy and contentment? Have you cried out to the Lord and asked for His joy to fill your heart? If not, do so now through a spoken prayer or by writing your request in a note to the Lord.

   _____
   _____
   _____

3. When you consider the joys of heaven, what do you look forward to most?

   _____
   _____
   _____

4. Spend some quality time with the Lord, asking Him to reveal to you in a personal way how the knowledge of the joy that awaits you in heaven can make your times of suffering and sadness here on earth more tolerable.

_____

_____

_____

5. Do you know someone who is going through a difficult time right now? Does he or she know the Lord and His promise that joy will come in the morning? If not, take some time to write him or her a note or give him or her a call to share this marvelous truth. Be sure and share from your own experience how Jesus has brought you joy through pain.

_____

_____

_____

Chapter Six

Packing for the Journey

> *Then Jesus said, "Come to me, all of you who are weary and carry heavy burdens, and I will give you rest. Take my yoke upon you. Let me teach you, because I am humble and gentle at heart, and you will find rest for your souls. For my yoke is easy to bear, and the burden I give you is light."*
> —Matthew 11:28-30 (NLT)

Friends, I would like you to think about how you pack for a trip. How many of us can honestly say that we use at least once every single item we pack and that we wear every article of clothing and every pair of shoes? How many of us find in an emergency that nothing in our many pounds of baggage will help?

Well, if you're anything at all like me, you fail miserably on all these counts! Despite thousands of miles of international travel, I am confident I have to be one of the world's worst packers! Traveling light, a highly recommended yet not easily attainable accomplishment, is something I just can't seem to achieve despite my best efforts. Just to give you an example, one time in the Malawi airport as I began my journey home from a summer in Africa, I was told by the airlines that I absolutely could not take all my baggage with me to London and then on to Los Angeles. It simply could not be done. There was too much, and it was far too heavy.

Here I was, halfway around the world, staring at my bags and wondering how I would ever get them home. The only solution was to find someone who would check one of my bags on their ticket to London (yes, this was many years before 9/11!). I would then have to retrieve it and recheck it to Los Angeles during the layover. Thankfully, I found a willing Malawian gentleman who was traveling with only a carry-on, and he, for a small fee, of course, checked one of my bags under his name, and my problem was solved.

You know, we stand on the threshold of eternity with oh so much baggage—anger, bitterness, resentment, unforgiveness—and the heavy burden of those things threatens to keep us from completing the journey to our heavenly home. There's just so much, and it can be so very heavy. But, thankfully, there is not just a man, but a Savior, who takes not just one of our bags, but all of our baggage, and He checks it under His name, the Lord Jesus Christ. And then He washes all that dirty, disgusting baggage with His blood and restores us to a wholeness of spirit and heart that enables us to travel lightly into God's presence. And you know what? He doesn't ask for a fee, not like the man in Malawi asked of me; He asks only for our acceptance of Him and His gift of grace, and for our love and obedience.

It's difficult to hand over that baggage to Him, though, isn't it? But we must! We need not bear the weight of all that. There is a way to pack for the journey that ensures we can indeed travel light! I have discovered a variety of tips that "guarantee" a traveler could journey lightly to anywhere in the world, and interestingly enough, I believe there are spiritual parallels to those tips.

1. **Once packed, don't repack**. Oh my goodness! How many hours have I spent repacking the items in my suitcase only to end up with them packed pretty much like they were at the beginning? What a waste of time and energy! The same is true of our spiritual lives. Once we are in possession of the truth, we must not waver. When we come to Jesus and recognize Him as our Lord and Savior, there is no need to look any further. People who are constantly changing their minds and repacking before a trip are like those who, even though they have met Jesus, are distracted and influenced by fads and trends and even fall victim to cults. Dear friends, once you have the truth, hang on to it; the truth of Jesus' kingship is all you will ever need on your journey heavenward if you have girded yourself with it.

2. **Pack things that don't get wrinkled**. Like fabrics that are easily mussed and wrinkled, our hearts are easily wrinkled by despair, discouragement, and temptation. What we need to pack is something that will protect

our hearts and keep them safe from the enemy's fiery darts as well as from our fears and insecurities. A breastplate of righteousness cannot be wrinkled and gives our vulnerable hearts the protection they need.

3. **Be prepared for emergencies**. The lists I found all suggested a variety of items to pack that would help us deal with unforeseen circumstances. Instead of all that, how about packing just one item—a sword? The sword of the Spirit, which is the Word of God, equips us to meet any emergency with His grace and power.

4. **Know where you're going**. Of course, the lists I found meant having maps and guidebooks. But we, as Christians, know that our feet already know the way because they are shod with the preparation of the gospel of peace.

5. **Protect yourself**. Here, the lists I found recommended vitamins, antacids, antibacterial hand wash, and many other items designed to keep us safe and healthy. But hey, instead of packing an entire pharmacy (that's got to

be heavy!), how about simply packing the shield of faith? After all, it's designed by God's power to protect us from anything harmful!

6. **Don't lose your passport**. Having lost my passport once while boarding a plane in Zurich, I know how wise this advice is for our earthly travels. But for our journey toward eternity and the heavenly mansion our Father has prepared for us, we have a passport that can't be lost. The helmet of salvation, purchased with the blood of Christ, gives us passage into God's presence.

Hm . . . does any of this sound familiar? Yes, all we need to pack for our journey is listed in Ephesians 6. The armor of God will guarantee our safe passage, and we don't even need a giant suitcase to pack it in. All we need are open, willing hearts.

Okay, so now that we have an idea of how to lighten our load and how to more efficiently pack for our journey, let's talk for a minute about *why* it so important not to be dragging enormous pieces of baggage that are stuffed full of heavy burdens.

The most important reason I can think of is this: if I am dragging around a giant suitcase crammed full of heavy stuff I have no need for, it takes a great deal of time and energy and leaves me unable to do anything else. Those heavy burdens we haul around in our hearts and minds render us incapable of fulfilling our roles in God's kingdom. They simply leave us too exhausted to minister.

Several years ago I experienced the excruciating pain of sciatica, which rendered me unable to move, and with soaring blood pressure. This condition had escalated over a few days and finally, after midnight one night, I succumbed and called my dear friend, Tricia. She immediately came to my home and promptly called 911 for medical assistance. The firefighters who responded were efficient and businesslike, but warm in their treatment of me. There was one, however, a young man training to be a fireman-paramedic, who was particularly attentive. He rode in the ambulance with me, held my hand, and tried to make me laugh through my tears. At the hospital, even though his duties were complete once I was handed over to the care of the emergency room staff, he went in search of a warm blanket, covered me up, and stayed by my side until Tricia had arrived.

After a couple of hours, and examinations too numerous to recount, I was given an injection and Tricia took me home. For the first time in many days I was able to sleep relatively pain-free. I awoke in the morning just wanting to sing, "Thank you, Lord, for the wisdom you instill in doctors and nurses, and for the compassion of sweet, gentle firefighters!"

The remedy did not last, however, and several days later I was again incapacitated by pain and out-of-control blood pressure. It was noon and another friend, Mary Jean, had arrived at my home to take me to a doctor's appointment. Oh my goodness! I was still in my jammies and absolutely unable to move. For the second time in five days, 911 was called on my behalf, and soon another group of firefighters arrived to provide medical transport. This time there was an older member of the group who showed an extraordinary amount of care and concern for me. He also held my hand, spoke encouraging and uplifting words with a quiet but authoritative voice, and even laughed at the crazy, nonsensical jokes I made in a desperate effort to keep the overwhelming ocean of pain from drowning me.

Those two encounters with the different shifts of firefighters not only provided the essential service of swift and safe transportation to the hospital but encouraged and cheered me as well. I was very grateful for their assistance and care.

The day after my second trip to the hospital emergency room, Tricia called me on the phone. She said, "I know you haven't felt up to reading your newspaper lately, but I wanted to let you know that there is something you need to be aware of in the paper this morning." She proceeded to tell me that four firefighters had been killed when the private plane they were flying in en route to a mountain ski trip had crashed. There were pictures of the four firefighters in our local paper, and when Tricia had seen them, she immediately recognized one of the victims as the young fireman-paramedic-in-training who had been so kind to me on my midnight journey to the emergency room. Little did she know that when I looked at the pictures in the newspaper I would recognize not only that young man but also the older firefighter who had also been so sweet and encouraging.

I was devastated. I couldn't imagine how painful this news must have been for their young families and for their colleagues at the firehouse they were assigned to. I prayed fervently for comfort and peace to envelop all who were grieving their loss. I also prayed for some measure of understanding . . . what possible good could come from this tragedy? It was then that I realized if these men had been dragging around hearts and minds crammed full of heavy burdens, they would not have been able to minister to me like they had. They would have simply done their job and not gone the extra mile. But because they were traveling light, they touched my life in a unique and special way. They brought light to a darkness I thought would never break, they brought comfort to a body wracked with pain, and they brought hope when I wanted to give up.

How grateful I am that they were traveling light when their lives touched mine. Their kindnesses, coupled with their tragic deaths, reminded me in a poignant and painful way of just how tenuous is this hold we have on life. We have no idea when the

Lord will call us home, so we need to take every opportunity we're presented with to be Christ to the people we encounter in our daily lives. We can't do that if we are saddled with the excessive baggage of emotional scars, resentment, anger, guilt, jealousy, unforgiveness, and the like. As we pack for the journey of life, we need to forgo these heavy burdens that weigh us down and weaken our capacity for ministry. We have a job to do for the glory of our Lord and the good of His kingdom! Our being prepared to minister with those God puts in our path allows us to gift them with their own "hallelujah moment" and makes a glorious difference in eternity!

Another Step Further

1. What heavy "stuff" is weighing you down and taking up valuable time and energy as you lug it around? Write a list of those heavy burdens. Now read 1 Peter 5:7. Go through your list and verbally, out loud, cast each of those burdens on the Lord. When you've gone through your entire list, have a celebratory cup of tea and rejoice in the fact that your precious Lord and Savior cares for *you!*

   _____

   _____

   _____

2. Has there been a time in your life when you were so heavily burdened that you were unable to minister in the manner God desired? How did you handle that situation? Did you just try to forget it, or did you ask for the Lord's forgiveness? Ask for His forgiveness now if you haven't done so already. He will answer you with the gift of a lightened heart and an increased capacity for ministry.

   _____

   _____

   _____

3. Read Matthew 11:28-30. How does obedience lighten your load? In what ways can you be more obedient to the Lord's commands and therefore prepare yourself to reach out to others more effectively?

_____

_____

_____

4. Celebrate the truth of Psalm 147:3. How has the Lord healed your broken heart and bound up your wounds? Think of someone you know who is struggling and broken and wounded—make a commitment to yourself and to the Lord to reach out to that person with the good news of His unconditional love and His ability to heal.

_____

_____

_____

5. When you consider your journey of life, what size suitcase are you hauling around with you? How can you effectively downsize? Where will you go and what will you do with your newly lightened heart?

   _____
   _____
   _____

Chapter Seven

Out of the Mouths of Babes

Then He said, "I tell you the truth, you must change and become like little children. Otherwise, you will never enter the kingdom of heaven."
—Matthew 18:3 (NCV)

During the month of October, all the classes at my school study community helpers. One of my jobs as a speech-language pathologist is simply to build vocabulary. One day I was working with a group of children and had large pictures of a fire truck and firefighter, a police car and a police officer, and a hospital with doctors and nurses. I was talking to the children about the jobs of each of these community helpers—a firefighter puts out fires, doctors and nurses take care of us when we're sick, and police officers keep us safe.

During this whole discussion, one of the little boys was looking quite skeptical—not when I was talking about the firefighter or the doctor and nurse but when I was talking about the police officer and his job of keeping us safe. His eyebrows were raised, and he was looking at me with a very critical eye. At the end of the lesson, I asked as a means of review, "Who puts out fires?" There was a loud chorus of "firefighters" from the children. I asked, "Who takes care of us when we are sick or hurt?" Their little voices sang out, "Doctors and nurses!" Finally I asked, "And who keeps us safe?" All of the children with the exception of the one skeptical little fellow shouted, "Police officers!" Then after his friends' voices had died out, this little guy looked at me very earnestly and said, "Oh no, Miss Jane, *God* keeps us safe!"

How I love to find God's glory reflected in children! The instructional assistant who had been sitting with my group was moved to tears, and so was I, not only by the impact of this sweet little boy's words but even more so by the conviction and passion with which he spoke them. All day I kept thinking about that incident and praying that the Lord would someday find in me that same conviction and that same passion so that I might be as effective as this little one in reflecting God's glory to a hurting world.

My great-niece Emma, at the tender age of seven, has become quite an accomplished swimmer. When she was first learning how to swim, her parents would frequently review what she had learned in her lessons. One day her mother asked her, "Now, Emma, what would you do if you fell in the pool?" Hoping for an answer that listed the steps she had learned in her swimming class, Mama Andrea was surprised (but delighted!) when Emma replied, "I'd pray for help!"

Oh, if only our first response to trials and tribulations would be prayer! How much time do we spend running around like the proverbial chicken with its head cut off, frantically trying to "fix" things, when what we really need to do is take a moment to breathe deeply, focus on our precious Lord, speak to Him about our concerns, and then stop and *listen* for His reply. We would save ourselves a whole lot of heartache and frustration if we would just go to Him first, confident that He will give us the guidance and protection that we need.

We can't bring glory to our Lord and Savior in any more effective ways than these two children have exemplified. We bring great glory to Him when we boldly proclaim His power *and* when we confidently put our trust in Him during our darkest hours. I think our Lord Himself must have "hallelujah moments" when we give up trying to manage the circumstances of our lives ourselves and finally rest in His wisdom and power.

Another Step Further

1. Read 2 Corinthians 3:18 and 2 Thessalonians 1:12. How have you reflected the Lord's glory today? Think about how your day has gone—what exactly did you reflect to the people who crossed your path? Frustration, anger, insecurity, downright grumpiness? How could your reflection have been more Christlike? What can you do to change your reflection?

   _____

   _____

   _____

2. There was a refrigerator magnet I saw once that said, "Dear child, I can do it myself. Love, God." What does this tell us about how our Lord feels when we try to forge ahead with our own plans and agendas without consulting Him? What can you do to ensure your commitment to a "pray first" attitude when it comes to handling difficult decisions or situations?

   _____

   _____

   _____

3. When was the last time you boldly proclaimed the might and majesty of the Lord? Who in your life needs to know they have a Savior who loves them unconditionally? Make plans right now to take those people to lunch, call them on the phone, or write them a note. Commit yourself to letting them know in no uncertain terms that they are loved by the Creator of the universe. Be prepared to share with them the blessings that you enjoy because of the love of the Father.

   _____
   _____
   _____

4. Guess what, dear ones—this life we have is not about us, it's about *Him!* How can you reflect this concept in your everyday life? What things do you need to change in your lifestyle? How can you reflect the glory of the Lord with actions and not words?

   _____
   _____
   _____

5. Read Psalm 18:2. Is the Lord truly your rock and your fortress, or do you rely on your own devices to handle the circumstances of life? When friends, family, coworkers, or acquaintances observe how you handle a difficult situation, what do they see? Do they see someone who relies only on herself or himself, or do they see someone whose strength comes from his or her trust and faith in the Lord Jesus Christ?

_____

_____

_____

Chapter Eight

Whom Do You Trust?

Depend on the Lord and his strength; always go to him for help.
—1 Chronicles 16:11 (NCV)

Many years ago, I was privileged to travel to Romania as a member of a disability ministry outreach team organized by Joni and Friends[2]. We spent the first few days ministering in Bucharest, and then the larger team was assembled into smaller, more focused teams, each headed to a separate city to provide concentrated training regarding a variety

---

[2] Joni and Friends is an international ministry dedicated to extending the love and message of Jesus Christ to people who are affected by disability around the world. Learn more about this incredible outreach at www.joniandfriends.org.

of disability-related issues. I was part of the team designated for ministry in the city of Oradea. The journey to this picturesque city in the region of Transylvania (seriously!) required a plane ride on the Romanian national airlines.

I suspected this would be an eventful journey when we arrived at the airport and procured our plane tickets. They were handwritten on newsprint! This did not bode well for modern travel amenities. As we walked outside the terminal across the tarmac, one of the gentlemen on our team advised me not to look at the tires of the plane we were headed toward. Of course, I looked! Much to my dismay, even I could tell the tires were worn beyond acceptable safety standards. The tires were not just bald, there was mesh showing through!

After boarding the plane, this gentleman and I chose seats in the very front of the plane. While there were many Romanian nationals on this flight, our group was also substantial in number. We were soon hearing sighs of frustration and nervous laughter as some of our team discovered their seat belts were either missing or nonfunctional. As I faced forward, trying to make sense of this breach in airline safety measures, I noticed that an exit door located toward the cockpit was secured with what appeared to be twine—and not even what I would describe as strong or thick twine! Then my eyes fell on the interior of the cockpit. I was afraid to even surmise why a couple of brown glass bottles, the kind that beer is often bottled in, had been abandoned on the instrument panel.

The plane took off, and as the journey got underway, I was expecting the customary safety lecture presented by the flight attendants. Well, there was only one flight attendant on this very large plane, and she wasn't talking. Not a word. I looked above to locate the apparatus that will descend in emergencies to provide a needed oxygen supply . . . nonexistent. This was not a comforting thought, as the air circulation in the plane's cabin was already not what it should be.

As the plane ascended and then leveled off for the duration of the flight, I began to question if the pilot was reading the altimeter correctly—or if the plane even had a functional altimeter at all. Peering out the window, I could see we were not flying over the Carpathian Mountains, we were skimming them! Now, I know this may seem to be an exaggeration, but really, if I could have opened a window and reached out my hand, I could have easily touched the tops of the trees!

Then the time came for our in-flight beverage and snack service. The "snack" on this flight was unique, to say the least. No pretzels or peanuts to be had here, oh no. Our treat was a tiny little "guma"—gumball! And believe you me, it was as hard as a rock! No human person on this earth could possibly have saliva with oomph enough to soften one of those!

After the guma had been passed out, the lone flight attendant began to distribute the beverage (note this word is singular)—there was no choice involved in the beverage service. She was holding a small tray with probably eight cups on it and was filling the cups with bottled water. The plane was so hot, I gratefully took the cup that was offered and sipped on the water, but within just a couple of minutes this lady had the tray in front of me again and was indicating that I needed to return the cup. Okaaaaay . . . seemed a little strange to me, but after one last swallow, I returned the cup, with some water still remaining in it, to the tray. You can imagine my surprise when the flight attendant, having reacquired the cups she had previously distributed, began to refill them! Then she moved down a couple of rows, offering the cups to the next travelers. Yikes! Members of our team who had been observing this water distribution alternated between gasping in dismay and giggling uncontrollably. None of us had ever seen anything like it! Later that evening, when this unconventional flight was being discussed, I reflected that I was glad about being in the front row—at least I was the first person to drink from the cup! Someone on the team brought me back to reality, however, by commenting, "How many flights do you think those cups have been on since they were washed?"

Wow! This was, hands down, the most memorable flight I have ever been on. I doubt there will ever be one to top it and hope there never will be! As the flight progressed, I began to fret with fervency. *We're in the air, we seem to be making forward progress, but are we really heading to Oradea? When, and if, we get there, is the plane going to land safely?* I can't begin to tell you the number of gruesome scenarios my mind conjured up in a matter of a few minutes. The "what-ifs" were horrifying!

As my imagination spiraled out of control, the gentlemanly team member I was sitting next to took my hand. How blessed I was to be sitting next to someone who was so remarkably perceptive. I thought I was hiding my growing panic pretty well, but apparently the fact that I was on the edge of hysteria was obvious to him. I wonder if it was the sweat pouring out of me or the fact that I was shaking uncontrollably that led him to conclude I needed help. Perhaps it was the prompting of the Holy Spirit; but for whatever reason, this kindly man began to pray, and while I cannot remember the exact words of his prayer, what I do remember very distinctly is the sense of peace that flooded my soul.

I realized I was in a crisis of trust! I most definitely did not trust the plane or the pilots' abilities, but, in actuality, was our safe arrival in Oradea really up to them? No! As it always has been and ever shall be, the Lord and only the Lord held our safekeeping in His hands. Whether or not we arrived at our earthly destination or a heavenly one, it was the Creator of the universe who was in control and who would, in the event of catastrophe, work even that for the good of His kingdom. I hope, dear friends, that you believe beyond a shadow of a doubt that our good and gracious Lord can turn any event or circumstance into a "hallelujah moment" if we simply put our trust in Him.

Another Step Further

1. Read Psalm 20:7, Psalm 40:4, Psalm 56:3, Psalm 118:8, and Proverbs 28:26. Whom do you trust? When fear, anxiety, apprehension, and worry flood your soul and threaten to undermine your peace of mind, what is your response? Do you turn to the things and people of the world, or do you put your trust in the Lord?

   _____

   _____

   _____

2. Read Psalm 13:5. What does the phrase "unfailing love" mean to you? How have you experienced God's unfailing love? Have you shared those experiences with anyone? If not, commit yourself to bringing hope and encouragement to someone struggling by sharing how your trust in the Lord's unfailing love made a difference in your life.

   _____

   _____

   _____

3. Read John 14:1. One of the most difficult things to do while living in this fallen world is to obey this Scripture and not allow our hearts to be troubled. What do you find most troubling about our world and about your life in particular? When you notice your heart becoming increasingly troubled, how can you keep those feelings from escalating? Make a list of things you can do to put the brakes on troubling thoughts and accelerate your trust in your Lord and Savior.

_____

_____

_____

4. Read Romans 15:13. How does trusting in God give you hope? Is there someone you know who is living in a hopeless state? How can you help him or her understand that trusting in the Lord will result in the joy and peace he or she longs for?

_____

_____

_____

5. We often hear about people having "trust issues" with regard to other people. But many people in our society have "trust issues" with God. Why do you think that is? What can you do to help those folks understand that our Lord is completely trustworthy? Share examples from your own life when yes, indeed, your trust in people was misplaced and disastrous but your trust in the Lord was blessed beyond expectation.

_____
_____
_____

Chapter Nine

The Hope of Heaven

Then will the eyes of the blind be opened and the ears of the deaf unstopped. Then will the lame leap like a deer, and the mute tongue shout for joy.
—Isaiah 35:5-6a (NIV)

Geoff was a star athlete in his high school, a popular and bright young man with an exciting future ahead of him. He loved the Lord and was actively involved with his church's youth group. He was being recruited by a variety of college football coaches. But during the final game of his senior season he was hit broadside by another player. As he lay on the field, no one thought to remove his helmet and his head swelled dramatically. His helmet had to be cut off. As a result, Geoff was severely brain-injured. He cannot walk without assistance, and he has a speaking vocabulary that is generally limited to a few pet phrases. His mother must assist him with every activity of daily life.

I was blessed to meet Geoff and his mother in Florida when I was serving as volunteer coordinator at a Joni and Friends family retreat for families experiencing disability. The next summer, we were together again at the JAF family retreat in North Carolina. On a hot August night, I sat next to Geoff during a chapel service, and as the worship leader led the assembly in singing wonderful old hymns about heaven, I suddenly became very aware of Geoff. In a voice nothing less than angelic, with tears streaming down his face, he was singing each and every word of those hymns.

I was amazed! Here was a young man who, for all intents and purposes, has lost everything—his abilities, his potential, his future—and yet he was singing praises to the Lord without missing a beat. How could this be? Well, there is something Geoff has not lost—the Holy Spirit! As Geoff sang that night, it was obvious to all who were around him that the Spirit was present indeed. While Geoff may have lost everything the world considers important, he still has the only thing of real significance in his life—faith in his heavenly Father. Geoff has lost nothing of eternal consequence. His unwavering focus is on heaven.

Dear friends, I have a question for you . . . how often, and how intently, do *you* focus on heaven? What do you envision when you think about heaven: A release from earthly trials? A reunion with friends and loved ones who have gone before? Theological debates with the prophets and apostles? I guess I find myself in the "release from earthly trials" camp—no more tears or sorrow or pain. In thinking about heaven, I always assumed that people struggling with disabilities and terminal illnesses would think about it in pretty much the same terms—as a release from their earthly infirmities and a joyous fulfillment of Isaiah's words as they stand whole and complete in the presence of their God and Father.

But through the years I have learned that, yes, my friends are looking forward to having legs that run and ears that hear and eyes that see, but those things pale in the light of being able to worship and praise our Lord Jesus face-to-face and thank Him for the grace and strength that made it possible for them to endure life on earth. Many years ago, as we sat sweltering in a church in Bucharest, Romania, Joni Eareckson Tada taught me an incredible lesson about heaven. She said that the first thing she wants to do with her new body when she gets to heaven is not to run and jump and hug but rather to *kneel* before her Lord and Savior Jesus Christ in gratitude for His gift of eternal life and for His unconditional and immeasurable love that made that gift possible.

We have an incredible responsibility as the body of Christ to those who struggle in this earthly life with disability and disease, a responsibility to set the stage for that glorious day when they will know firsthand the awesome meaning behind Isaiah's words in chapter 35. We must make the love of our Lord Jesus Christ accessible to all. We must share the hope of heaven and focus their thoughts (and ours too!) not on earthly trials and tribulations but rather on the ultimate newness that will be ours in heaven. We need to be sensitive to the opportunities we have every day to make a difference, the *eternal* difference, in the lives of families experiencing disability or disease. We are blessed with the privilege of letting them know the simple but powerful truth—that Jesus was disabled on the cross so that we could be able in heaven.

How we live our lives now, here on earth, will make a difference in how we spend eternity. Are you willing to use the gifts and abilities that God has blessed you with to give those who are suffering a taste of heaven? Are you willing to share the hope of heaven with families who desperately need that hope? While it is indeed important that we strive to meet the practical needs of such families by providing respite care, cooking meals, cleaning house, doing laundry, providing transportation, and the like, there is great danger in ministry that remains earthbound, concerned only with meeting immediate needs. We must point the people God brings into our lives heavenward, and sometimes that is very difficult to do.

Several years ago, Steve Hammer, now Lead Pastor of Impact Christian Church in Moon Township, Pennsylvania (and alumnus of the same high school as me—go Patriots!), the brother of a dear friend, wrote an extraordinary letter to his daughter, Cayla. He had written a special letter to Cayla on the day she was born, just like he had for each of her two big sisters, and now he has written a second letter—not to mark the occasion of her graduation or engagement or marriage, as you might expect, but as part of the healing process after her death.

In his letter, Steve wrote,

> When the doctors told us you were dying, Mommy and I didn't know how to tell you. We wanted to talk to you but we didn't want to confuse you. We didn't know what to say, so we asked God to talk to you, and to give us wisdom. You were hurting so badly that we began praying that you would go quickly.
>
> The doctors told us you could hear me, so I talked to you about how nice heaven was going to be. How there would be no needles, no medicine, and no more chemo. I told you that Jesus would take good care of you in heaven, and that He loved you even more than Mommy and I. I told you that we would not be mad at you if you

went to heaven, and that we would join you there someday.

I was glad when Grandma and Grandpa told us that while Mommy and I were out of the room, you had been talking to God. They told us that you talked about a nice man who wanted you to go to His house with Him. They told us that you said He was like your daddy but that He wasn't your daddy. It is so comforting to know that while we were urging you to heaven from this side, Jesus was calling you from His side.

But Cayla, we miss you so much. I keep thinking of all the things I will never see you do . . . I'll never see you ride a bike or go to kindergarten or graduate or get married. But there are other things I will never have to see: I'll never see you skin your knee, or cry from a broken heart, or suffer from your own sin. I'll never again wait for you to come out of surgery, or hold your hand while they put a needle in your little body. We miss the good times, but we are so glad that your bad times are over for eternity.

And the best part is, we will see you again. We will see you in heaven. We will see you smile, hear you laugh, and join you as you sing praises to Jesus.

How lucky we are that God gave you to us! We are so anxious to come to heaven to be with you. Until we do, we will keep loving Jesus. I will keep preaching and trying to help others to accept God's gift of forgiveness and heaven . . . and honey, your daddy is not yet like the Man who was calling you, but I will spend the rest of my life trying to be like Him.

We'll see you soon. Mommy and I look forward to holding you in heaven.

All my love always,
Daddy

How was Steve able to write this? How was he able to let go of his precious little one? How has he been able to go on? How is he able, even now, to significantly impact the lives of all those around him? Because even in the midst of the most painful loss of his life, he has never forgotten that He is one of God's chosen, holy and dearly loved, and because every day, even before putting on the armor of God, he clothes himself with compassion, kindness, gentleness, and patience. He wears the glorious adornment of a man who loves and serves Christ Jesus *and* who clings to the hope of heaven with tenacity and fervor. He believes with all his heart that when his earthly journey is done, he will be reunited with Cayla and spend eternity with her in the presence of his God and King. The hope of heaven sustains him and gives his life purpose. It is a lifeline when the circumstances of life threaten to drown him.

When my great-niece Kailie Jane was three years old, she announced one night at the dinner table that she needed a ladder. When her parents asked her why on earth she needed a ladder, she said, "I want to climb up to heaven to see Grandpa Jim Pom-Pom!" This precious little girl had never met her great-grandfather (my father) on earth, but from what she was learning from family stories about his great love, she was sure he was someone she wanted to know and that heaven was the place to be for that to happen. Kailie Jane has been told since before she was born that Grandpa Jim Pom-Pom loves her even though he hasn't met her yet. So she was ready and willing to ascend an incredibly tall ladder to get to the prize of a face-to-face encounter with him.

How willing are we to make whatever climb is necessary to reach the One who has known and loved us since before we were born? There is no doubt that giving up the ways of the world and completely relinquishing control of our lives to our Lord and Savior is a difficult uphill climb. But we know, beyond a shadow of a doubt, that the delight of meeting our Lord and Savior face-to-face and the joy of spending eternity praising Him far outweigh the struggle of the climb. It will probably be a long time before Kailie Jane gets to heaven and meets Grandpa Jim Pom-Pom, but in the meantime she will be learning all she can about him and eagerly anticipating their meeting. Likewise, it may be awhile before we get to heaven and have that first incredible face-to-face encounter with our Redeemer. Meanwhile, are we learning everything we can about Him through His Word? Are we living our lives in eager anticipation of the coming glory? Is the hope of heaven a reality we reflect in our daily lives? Are you sharing the "hallelujah moments" of your lives so that others may know Jesus and desire to meet Him? I pray, dear ones, that you are doing *all* these things in celebration of heaven's "hallelujah moments" to come!

Another Step Further

1. Read Colossians 3:1-4. What can you do to keep your focus on the "things in heaven" rather than on the "things on earth"? How will this focus help you deal with the trials and tribulations of everyday life?

   _____
   _____
   _____

2. Read Isaiah 35:5-6a. What is the promise contained in this passage of Scripture? What does this promise mean to you personally? Who do you know who needs the encouragement found in this passage? Make a commitment right now to share that promise with him or her through a phone call, written note, or better yet, a personal visit.

   _____
   _____
   _____

3. Read John 14:2-4. Jesus says, "You know the way to where I am going" (NCV). What is "the way" He is referring to? Are you on the way—wholeheartedly and without reservation?

___

4. Read Colossians 3:12. How does this spiritual clothing give you the strength to keep focused on the glory to come? How can being clothed in compassion, kindness, humility, gentleness, and patience prepare you to share the hope of heaven with others?

___

5. Read Revelation 21:4-8. This passage of Scripture contrasts the hope of heaven with the eternal punishment of the unrepentant. Yikes! Who do you know who needs to face the reality of what is described in this passage? How can you boldly but lovingly share this truth with

that person? Make a commitment to not only share the truth of this passage, but to encourage and uplift this person as he or she strives to change his or her life for his or her own good and for the good of the kingdom.

_____
_____
_____

Chapter Ten

In Memoriam

James Ward Simmons
April 26, 1931–November 19, 2006

My father was a quiet, gentle man. In my entire life, I only heard him raise his voice twice—and both times it was directed at my whackadoodle dog! He never spoke harshly to anyone, and he never laid a hand on us except to tickle or hug us. As a small child, one of my favorite daily events was exiting the bathtub dripping wet and running to him where he waited with a towel. He would proclaim every single time as he dried me off and got me into my pajamas, "You are squeaky clean!" I felt loved and accepted and cherished after that proclamation. That daily event was one of the highlights of my childhood, and I realize now it was a little taste of heaven. I am so looking forward to the day when I stand before my Father in heaven who will proclaim me not only "squeaky clean," thanks to the sacrifice of His Son, but loved and accepted and cherished as His daughter!

Daddy was just about as kind and gentle and soft-spoken as a man could be, but believe you me, he was no slacker in the discipline department! We daughters of his knew the rules of the house, we knew the boundaries for our behavior, and we (pretty much) toed the line. In particular, we knew that under no circumstances would talking back to our mother or failing to get home on time be tolerated.

When we did disobey or step out of line, we weren't called out in public or in front of the rest of the family, we weren't chastised or reprimanded with cruel words, and we weren't made to feel shame or embarrassment. We were simply called into his home office. It was with great trepidation that I made that journey into his office on, unfortunately, more than one occasion. I would sit down at the desk opposite his and await his words. He would always calmly and quietly explain why I was there, give me a chance to plead my case and eventually express my remorse, and then announce a just and reasonable consequence.

When I left his office, I always thought to myself, *Oh man, I am never going to do that again!* But I knew that if I did do whatever it was again, Daddy would patiently and lovingly help me see the error of my ways and gently nudge me in the direction of more respectful and appropriate behavior. What was always the absolute worst part of these little conferences was not the confession I had to make nor the consequences I had to face but the knowledge that I had disappointed Daddy.

Did my sister and I obey our father because we were afraid of him? No. Did we obey because we feared displeasing or disappointing him? Yes. Did we obey because we respected and honored him? Yes.

And so I began to learn from my earthly father what it meant to respect and honor my heavenly Father. What I learned was that I should desire more than anything else to please Him through my obedience. Just as I loved and honored my fleshly father, I was to love and honor my heavenly Father.

I was to obey God for the same reasons I obeyed Daddy. How sad I am that it took me long into my adult years to understand that! How I regret the time I spent as a rebellious young woman!

Through Daddy's example I also learned that when I disobeyed God, when I dishonored Him with my words and actions, that He would call me into His presence through the conviction of the Holy Spirit (just as Daddy had called me into his office). And just as Daddy had done with my childhood transgressions, the Lord would point out my sin; give me an opportunity to confess, repent, and seek His forgiveness; and then send me out to "go and sin no more." Wow! Daddy had the Lord's methodology down to a tee!

I know that I was abundantly blessed to have an earthly father who was a godly man, able to teach me what it means to revere and respect God. A few days after he had passed away, I went into his home office and took note of the three books that were on his desk—his Bible, a copy of Rick Warren's *The Purpose-Driven Life: What On Earth Am I Here for?* (Zondervan, 2002), and a copy of Oswald Chambers's *My Utmost for His Highest*

(Barbour Books, 1963). Anyone who went into that room would have known what kind of man he was simply by observing the selection of books on his desk.

How grateful I am that I was blessed with a father who loved the Lord, and who trusted Him and served Him with compassion, humility, and tender faith. This man who cried during *Fiddler on the Roof*[3] said he could really relate to Tevye and his exasperating daughters. He also cried during *E.T.: The ExtraTerrestrial*[4] and as result vowed he would never to let us pick a movie again because of it! This man who made great sacrifices to provide our family with all we needed and much, much more, this man who loved us all without reservation—son, husband, daddy, Grandpa Jim Pom-Pom—he

---

[3] Directed and produced by Norman Jewison, distributed by United Artists, released November 3, 1971.

[4] Directed by Stephen Spielberg, produced by Stephen Spielberg and Kathleen Kennedy, distributed by Universal Pictures, released June 11, 1982.

was a man who I believe, like David, was "a man after God's own heart."

As he advanced in age and friends and family members passed away after long illnesses or devastating battles with disease, he would often say, "I hope the good Lord takes me while I'm snoozin' in my own bed!" And that is exactly what happened. After baking lemon cookies with Mother and finishing a novel he had been reading, he closed his eyes in slumber only to open them, not to a crisp fall Idaho morning, but to behold his Lord and Savior face-to-face. And I believe beyond a shadow of a doubt that the first words he heard in his heavenly home were, "Well done, good and faithful servant."

Janet Louise (nee Beam) Simmons
January 8, 1931–November 26, 2011

My mother never met a stranger in her life. Wherever she would go in the community—to the doctor's office, to the market, to a restaurant—she would engage the people she met in conversation.

She was known for her outgoing friendliness and sense of humor. In short, she was a character!

A few years back, I was chaperoning a youth group overnighter, and in preparation I had filled the back of my car with an outlandishly enormous number of rolls of toilet paper. I thought that the age-old tradition of toilet papering an unsuspecting victim's front yard might help break the monotony of being locked down in the church building for over twelve hours. Much to my dismay, the members of the youth group were a bunch of total wimps! There was no convincing them that this would be fun. In fact, I think they were quite disturbed that I was an official "senior citizen" (fifty-five years old!) and encouraging them to participate in this raucous behavior. When I explained to them that it was *my mother* who taught my friends and me the fine art of toilet papering and, in fact, often drove our getaway car, they were appalled. Much to their credit, I have to admit, they never did give in, and there was no toilet papering that night. (A substantial donation of toilet paper was made to a shelter the following day, however!)

This is what I mean when I say my mother was a character. From late-night toilet-papering forays to boisterous singing with the player piano to midnight swims in our pool, she was always the life of the party. She was definitely the "hostess with the mostess"—and made a mean salsa from scratch. When guests would arrive at our home (always perfectly decorated for the season or the theme of the party), they would be greeted with the tantalizing aromas of only homemade dishes, warm hugs, and the guarantee of a rip-roarin' good time! And a good time would indeed be had by all, mostly because my mother told stories that could absolutely crack up even the sternest or most stoic of folks. Her stories were often self-deprecating but always hilarious; my mother just radiated cheer!

But she had a remarkably quiet and creative side as well. During our childhoods, my sister and I wore many a matching outfit, painstakingly created by our mother's hands. For quite some time, cross-stitching was her thing, and the pictures she produced are true works of art. The stitches are amazingly even and incomparable in their exact precision. Delicate and finely detailed, these masterpieces look as if they were produced by a machine rather than a human hand.

And then there are the quilts! What a legacy of love the members of my family and I have in the quilts that Mother produced. From the Christmas quilt that adorns my sister and brother-in-law's bed during the holidays to the apple quilt that commemorates my being named Teacher of the Year, these quilts are absolutely priceless. And she made these quilts to be used, not to just hang on a wall or sit in a cedar chest. I have one that has gone with me many times to camp, and we all have ones that have been used to construct living room forts or to comfort someone who is ill, and that have been spread on floors, carpets, pavement, and picnic areas to provide a cozy place to sit. These quilts are a poignant reflection of Mother's love. They would be invaluable no matter what, but in the case of Mother, they are particularly precious because it was so hard for her to verbally express how much she loved us. We knew we were deeply loved, but primarily through her creations and not through her words, and for the gift of these tokens of love we are all very grateful.

When remembering my mother in her role as hostess, storyteller, stitcher, and quilter extraordinaire, I can't help but ponder the contrast of that time of her life with her last few months on earth. Stricken with a debilitating spinal disease, she gradually lost the use of her legs and hands. This woman, who just weeks before had been driving her widowed lady friends to lunch sixty miles from home and roaming the aisles of Macy's, was struck down swiftly and completely. While her mind was fully intact, her physical body had failed her deplorably. This active, independent woman was suddenly bedridden and in excruciating pain. Our amazingly generous mother, Grandma Janet Gingo, and great-grandmother (known by her six great-grandchildren as "Great Janet") was wracked with pain so intense that she would sob uncontrollably.

Throughout this ordeal, she was understandably cranky and cantankerous. She was sometimes frustratingly mean and nasty. But throughout it all, she maintained her faith in a heavenly home that awaited her with a release from earthly suffering.

I don't know why our good and gracious Lord allowed her to suffer for those many weeks, but I suspect the lessons to be learned were for those of us who were left behind and not for her—lessons about maintaining graciousness in the midst of suffering, about dignity in dying, about trusting that our heavenly Father will indeed "wipe every tear from their eyes, and there will be no more death or sorrow or crying or pain . . ." (Rev. 21:4, NLT).

As the days approached for her homegoing, friends and loved ones who came to visit would encourage her heavenward by telling her that Daddy was waiting for her. We could just imagine him greeting her at the gates of heaven, saying, "Where have you been? I've been waiting for you!" The last understandable words she spoke were, "I'm sorry I'm late!" These words were spoken not with what sounded like frustration or anxiety over not meeting some timeline but rather with a sense of expectancy and exhilaration at finally arriving someplace that she had been trying very hard to get to for a very long time. We have no doubt she spoke those words to Daddy and to the Lord

Jesus Himself as they welcomed her to her heavenly home.

Less than twelve hours before she was released from earthly suffering, my sister and I received an e-mail from Christopher, my sister's youngest son. He wrote with such wisdom and clarity about a dream he had had upon returning to his home in Illinois after visiting his Grandma Janet Gingo in the last days of her life. He wrote in part,

> Grandma was sitting in her wheelchair in much the same condition as I saw her in while I was there to visit (very fragile and immobile-looking). Grandpa was sitting in a regular chair directly in front of her, facing toward her, and you two [my sister and I] were at each one of her sides with your hands resting on her shoulders . . . I recall there being a conversation between Grandma and Grandpa, which I don't remember being able to hear but could feel that he was trying to comfort her and convince her of something by the way he kept leaning forward to talk to her and placing his hand on her knee. At

the end, Grandpa stood up from his chair and took Grandma by the arms and helped her to her feet. They both stood there looking into each other's eyes and Grandma appeared to be in no pain at all. I remember waking up that morning with the same thought playing over and over in my head. We are not losing Grandma; we are simply returning her to Grandpa. Every time I get sad thinking about her, I tell myself the same thing. We are not losing her, we are reuniting her with Grandpa, and the sadness turns to joy. She will always be with us in our memories, and reunited with Grandpa, they will be looking out for us and our loved ones just as she and Grandpa always have.

How comforting I have found those words in the months since Mother passed. How blessed I am to know that amidst that "great cloud of witnesses" the apostle Paul wrote about, my mother stands, restored and renewed, cheering each member of our family on as they journey through life. I can hardly wait to see her again!

Richard Leon Beam
May 16, 1936–May 3, 2012

My uncle Dick was fifteen years old when I was born, and I was blessed to be the apple of his eye. There is a picture of us taken when I was not quite two, in a little blow-up kiddie pool. How many teenage boys do you know who would pose, let alone hang out and play in a kiddie pool, with a toddler? Well, my uncle Dick did! And that is just one of many examples of how I knew from a very early age that I was unabashedly adored.

Back in the '50s, long before seat-belt and car-seat laws were even considered, I would ride in the front seat of his car with him, standing as close to him as I possibly could with my arm wrapped around his neck. I don't remember where we went on those excursions, but I'm pretty sure that they frequently involved ice cream and a beautiful cheerleader named Dorothy.

Well, Dorothy eventually became my aunt Dorothy when she and Uncle Dick were married. At their wedding I thought I was the star of the show! I was nearly five, after all, and I was the flower girl—a very important person in my estimation! The only problem was that I was in such a rush to get down the aisle to my uncle Dick that I forgot to throw the flower petals!

As I grew older, Uncle Dick never failed to impress upon me the importance of education. From elementary school on, he always displayed a tremendous interest in my grades and courses of study, and he was a constant source of encouragement. He inspired me to choose a career in education, just as he had. Long before the law mandated that students with disabilities receive adaptive physical education instruction if needed, Uncle Dick chose to accept the assignment of teaching special education students how to swim when no one else would. That simple act had a tremendous impact on me. The unconditional love and genuine acceptance he had showered upon me since the day I was born was extended to these students whom the world saw as unworthy, unable to learn, and unlovable. But he saw them, not with the eyes of the world, but with the eyes of a man who looked on all people with a heart of compassion, respect, and tenderness.

With his passing, I know it will be a while before I see him again. But when I do, the countenance I behold will not be of a tired, broken body lying in bed wracked with pain; it will be of Uncle Dick, whole and complete, healed and restored. What a celebration heaven will be! Uncle Dick did not often profess his faith or feel the need to express verbally his belief in a heavenly Father and the future that awaits us in His kingdom, but the way he lived his life reflected this belief beyond any doubt.

He was a man of love—a man who loved and accepted people not because he had to, but because he chose to. He loved extravagantly and unreservedly. How blessed are we who were touched by that love that so reflects the love of our heavenly Father. Anyone whose life he touched is a better person for having known him and his kindness, generosity, and compassion.

When I spoke at his memorial service, I presented a challenge to the nearly five hundred people in attendance. I told them that it would not be enough to walk out of that sanctuary saying, "Yeah, that Dick Beam, he was a great guy!" No, that's simply not enough. I told them that if he had truly impacted their lives, then they should walk out of that sanctuary with a firm commitment to live their lives in a manner that shows the world that his life made a difference. The best way to honor his memory would not be to occasionally remember some kindness he extended or some goofy thing he did, but rather to live a life like he lived—loving your spouse and loving your kids, unabashedly adoring them so they don't have to go looking in all the wrong places for love and acceptance. Love education. Love those who are considered the least in our society. Love life. Live it with gusto, with passion, and with a heart of tenderness. That would truly honor the memory of Uncle Dick and, in turn, bring even greater honor and glory to our God in heaven.

Betty Eileen Blodgett
February 16, 1941-February 1, 2012

I don't recall the exact date I first had the privilege of meeting Betty Blodgett, the mother of my dear friend Christianne Lange. It seems like

Jane Lynn Simmons

I have always known her, that for as long as I can remember she was a special presence in my life.

Betty was always an incredible source of encouragement to me. I believe she was blessed with the gift of edification, at least as far as I was concerned. I never left an encounter with her without feeling uplifted and energized, ready to take on whatever was in store for me as I continued on life's journey.

To me, Betty embodied motherly love and concern, and there were many times I came away from a visit with her with my heart and soul renewed in the way only a mother can renew. With my own mother living in another state so far away, I have often had a mom-shaped hole in my heart that Betty's sweet spirit filled.

It was a constant source of joy to me to see the great admiration and pride with which Betty spoke of Christianne. She loved Christianne tremendously and took such joy from her accomplishments as a wife, mother, and Christian leader. She adored Tony as well, and her thankfulness at being blessed with a godly son-in-law was evident.

And oh, how she loved Abigail and Madeline! She was a grandmother in the truest sense of the word—she could brag with the best of 'em regarding her remarkable, beloved granddaughters and their talents.

Yes, Betty was a woman who loved immeasurably, and I am so very thankful that she shared that love with me.

Every time I think of you, I give thanks to my God.
—Philippians 1:3 (NLT)

Conclusion

What does it all mean, dear friends? Why is it important for us to rejoice and raise the roof with songs and praises for our God and King? Why must we not allow fear to incapacitate us, hindering the personal ministry we have been called to? Why must we run with endurance, rejoicing even in the midst of trials, and travel light on our journey through this world? Why must we recognize and celebrate the gifts and wisdom of our brothers and sisters who are considered "the least of these" by our fallen world? Why must we boldly proclaim the awesomeness of our Lord and adopt a "pray first" attitude? And why, oh why, must we trust God and God alone for our well-being and cling to His promise of eternity spent with Him in the glory of His kingdom?

The answer to these questions is a simple one—*because we have been commanded to do so* by our Lord and Savior, Jesus Christ. He clearly stated our responsibilities as God's children: "Jesus answered, 'Love the Lord your God with all your heart, with all your soul, and all your mind.' This is the first and most important command. And the second command is like the first: 'Love your neighbor as you love yourself'" (Matt. 22:37-39, NCV).

We are called to a life of faith. Not a faith that is static and fixed, but a faith that is vital, vivid, and very much engaged. A faith that motivates us to take opportunities as God presents them, to share the love of Jesus and the testimony of what He has done in our lives. Faith to invite the hurting and hopeless to church where they can experience the strength of a body united by the power of the Holy Spirit. Faith to encourage others to give themselves over to a lifesaving personal relationship with Jesus; and finally, faith to allow Christ Jesus to work through us in the lives of everyone we encounter.

This is the nature of the faith we are called to—the kind of faith that can, indeed, move mountains. When we trust God and abandon our lives to His mercy, He opens our eyes and hearts to those around us. I pray that the words you have read throughout this book have been a vehicle through which our awesome God has convicted you to bold action and extravagant love—and an enduring faith that touches His very heart.

Acknowledgments

To those of you who find yourselves within these pages, thank you. I hope you will find the words written here to be a unique and meaningful tribute to you and an expression of gratitude for the many ways in which you have enriched my life and drawn me closer to our Lord Jesus.

To those of you who read, and read, and then read some more, and who offered constructive and helpful input as the chapters were finished one by one, thank you. Sharon Bautista, Karen Clem, Ramona Cornejo, Lisa Dreher, Barbara Lewis, Jan List, Jean Minturn, Cindy Northcutt, Peggy Surman, Marcie Young—your enthusiasm for this project and your willingness to give of your own precious time to read made the process of writing much less solitary and far more enjoyable.

To my amazing family—Janis and Doug; Bryan, Andrea, Emma, and Caitlyn; Christopher, Jessica, Cole, Austin, Kailie Jane, and Rileigh—wow! How blessed I am to call you mine. Your constant love, support, encouragement, and inspiration have kept me going throughout the writing of this book. You've allowed me to be myself, quirky old gal that I am, and have been faithful to lift me up when discouraged and boot me further down the road when needed! Our family is small in number but mighty in love—and I know Grandpa Jim Pom-Pom and Great Janet share my immense pride in each of you. Thank you, from the bottom of my heart, for all that each of you does to reflect the love of Christ, not just to me, but to the people you meet in your everyday lives as well. May you find inspiration in this book for continued good works for the glory of God's kingdom.

About the Author

Jane Lynn Simmons is a native Californian, raised in Orange County. She holds a Bachelor of Arts Degree in Speech Pathology from La Verne College (1974) and a Master of Science Degree in Communicative Disorders with an emphasis in Language Pathology from the University of Redlands (1976). She has worked either as a Special Day Class teacher for students with communicative disorders or as a Speech-Language Pathologist for the past 35 years.

Jane has extensive experience in the field of disabilities ministry. In the 1980's she developed a cutting edge, internationally-recognized comprehensive ministry with families experiencing disabilities and has been a sought-after speaker/trainer regarding the church and disability. She has traveled the world in this capacity, consulting and training in Romania, Russia and China.

Other international experience includes mission work in Zambia and Panama. Jane has been a featured speaker and workshop leader at disability conferences throughout the United States. She has worked closely with Joni Eareckson Tada and her organization, not only in international outreach, but in the development of family retreats throughout the United States as well.

In recent years, Jane has been called to women's ministry. She has taught women's Bible studies in Irvine and Corona, California; has spoken at ladies' teas; and has been a featured speaker at women's retreats in California, Tennessee, Ohio, and Idaho.

Jane resides in Riverside, California, where she works as a Speech-Language Pathologist for Riverside Unified School District. She is a member of the Women's Ministry Council and serves as a women's Bible study teacher at Canyon Community Church of the Nazarene in Corona, California. Her spare time is spent reading, cross-stitching, and preparing dinners for family, friends, and colleagues.

CPSIA information can be obtained at www.ICGtesting.com
Printed in the USA
LVOW06s0056270713

344674LV00001B/48/P